*Brochis britskii,* Brazil

Other titles of interest:

The Tropical Aquarium
Community Fishes
Marine Fishes
Maintaining a Healthy Aquarium
Aquarium Plants
Central American Cichlids
Fish Breeding
African and Asian Catfishes
Koi
Livebearing Fishes
Fancy Goldfishes
Reptiles and Amphibians
Hamsters, Gerbils, Rats, Mice and Chinchillas
Rabbits and Guinea Pigs
Pet Birds
Softbills
Finches

# A FISHKEEPER'S GUIDE TO

# SOUTH AMERICAN CATFISHES

*Catfish in the community aquarium*

*Corydoras delphax*, Colombia

# A FISHKEEPER'S GUIDE TO

# SOUTH AMERICAN CATFISHES

Comprehensive advice on the care and breeding
of these intriguing fishes, featuring over 90 species

## David Sands

# Tetra Press

16036

# A Salamander Book

© 1988 Salamander Books Ltd.,
Published by Tetra Press,
201 Tabor Road,
Morris Plains, NJ 07950.

ISBN 3-923880-97-9

*Pimelodus pictus,* Peru and Colombia

## Credits
Editor: Anne McDowall    Design: Rod Ferring
Colour reproductions:
Contemporary Lithoplates Ltd.
Filmset: SX Composing Ltd.
Printed in Belgium by Henri Proost & Cie, Turnhout.

# Author

A combination of practical experience and academic research has made David Sands ideally qualified to present this survey of South American catfishes. As an importer and retailer of tropical freshwater and marine fishes, Mr Sands has encountered at first hand all the challenges which face the fishkeeper. Renowned internationally for his authoritative series of volumes on Catfishes of the World and a regular contributor to leading aquarist magazines in the UK and USA, he can advise both accomplished and aspiring fishkeepers how to keep and enjoy these intriguing fishes.

# Contents

Introduction 10

Selecting catfishes for the aquarium 12

Water requirements and filtration 22

Lighting and heating 28

Aquascaping 30

Feeding 34

Routine maintenance 38

Health care 40

Breeding 44

Species section 50
A photographic survey of over 90 South American catfishes

Index 114

Picture credits 117

Pages 10-11: *A typical habitat of South American catfishes*
Pages 50-51: *Sorubim lima*

# Introduction

Nowhere on earth rivals South America for its incredible variety of animal and plant life. Since this spectacular and diverse region also contains two thirds of the world's supply of fresh water, it is not surprising that its great rivers are the richest source of tropical fishes in the world.

Most rivers in South America hold a high number of catfish species and of the 14 South American catfish families, seven are well known to fishkeepers. These dominate over all other freshwater fish families, with the exception of characins (which include tetras, piranhas, hatchetfishes and pencilfishes).

The large catfishes of the mighty Amazon and Negro Rivers were among the first fishes encountered by 19th-century explorers, such as Bates and Darwin. It is probable that thousands of species of catfishes still remain to be discovered in the bountiful rivers of South America, rivers that begin their journey to

the sea in the high Andes, cascade over breathtaking waterfalls, thread across almost impenetrable rain forests, flow through swamps and spill onto the fringes of the coastal grasslands.

Although it is the Brazilian rivers of the Amazon Basin and the Matto Grosso that provide the great majority of catfish species available to fishkeepers, imports from Peru, Colombia, Guyana and Paraguay are also fairly common. Fishes from the bordering countries of Venezuela, Ecuador and Argentina, too, find their way into the tropical ornamental fisheries market.

The most common South American catfish is undoubtedly the archetypal 'whiskered' *Corydoras* (25-100mm/1-4in long). Other species, however, notably the 'Naked' Catfishes *Paulicea* and *Brachyplatystoma*, can eventually grow over 2m (6.5ft) long. Thus, South American catfishes, in so many shapes and sizes, provide enough variety to suit the interests of every fishkeeper.

# Selecting catfishes for the aquarium

There are South American catfishes to suit almost every style and size of aquarium, and the size of your tank will be the main factor in helping you decide which species to stock. Except in the case of large predatory catfishes, most species can be kept alongside other tropical fishes in a community aquarium. Nearly all catfishes live on the substrate and so will mix well with surface or middle water swimmers.

In this section we review the various types and sizes of catfishes available and the size of aquarium that will suit them best.

**Small, non-predatory catfishes**
Most fishkeepers have community systems, which include catfishes with other species of tropical freshwater fishes, and therefore need to distinguish between non-predatory and predatory fishes. Small, non-predators possess a mouth underneath the head, usually with downward-pointing barbels that allow the catfish to sift through the substrate for food. Here, we review a selection of small non-predatory catfishes in the major families.

**Callichthyidae** The first catfishes encountered by fishkeepers are usually *Corydoras*. This is principally because the bronze and albino varieties of the common *Corydoras aeneus* are

commercially farmed in North America and the Far East and are therefore readily available in aquarium shops.

There are over 100 species of *Corydoras*, a representative selection of which are dealt with in the species section. Any tropical freshwater community aquarium will be enchanced by the inclusion of these small armoured or plated catfishes, and even very modest-sized aquariums are suitable for keeping them. (See the table for recommended stocking levels.)

As these small catfishes live on the substrate, you could keep a trio of *Corydoras aeneus* together with a trio of *Corydoras paleatus* in a small community aquarium measuring 60x30x30cm (24x12x12in), without affecting the total number of fishes that can be kept in the tank. The close relatives of *Corydoras* – *Brochis* and *Aspidoras* – are available from time to time. You can safely keep these peaceful catfishes alongside their cousins and they will be equally compatible with other community fishes.

**Loricariidae** This is the largest family of catfishes in South

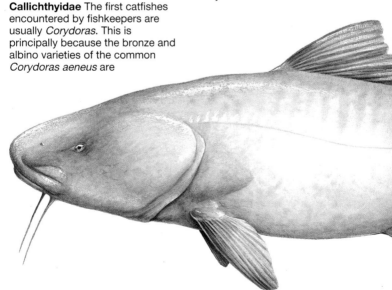

America, containing over 600 non-predatory species that range in size from 25mm (1in) to 750mm (30in). They are described as Suckermouths, Whiptails and Plecs, and are flattened in the body, often long and slender and, being poor swimmers, are ideal substrate fishes for a shallow community aquarium, i.e. with a depth of 30cm-38cm (12in-15in). However, some species, such as Twig Catfishes (*Farlowella*), prefer a deeper aquarium.

Certain catfishes from this family are ideal for the early days of a new aquarium – when the water is clean, the lights bright and

Below: *The variety of sizes of South American catfishes can be seen here. The sizes given are those of captive species, except* Paulicea *which is too large to be kept in the aquarium. Diminutive* Corydoras *are ideal for a small community, while the largest offer a challenge to the enthusiast.*

*Corydoras hastatus* (25mm/1in)

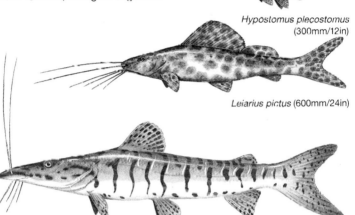
*Hypostomus plecostomus*
(300mm/12in)

*Leiarius pictus* (600mm/24in)

*Pseudoplatystoma fasciatum*
(900mm/36in)

*Paulicea sp.* (up to 2100mm/84in)

13

algae often turns the aquarium glass green. Your local retailer may be able to supply Bristle-nosed Catfishes (the common name given to many species of *Ancistrus*), which are efficient algae eaters. A further advantage of *Ancistrus* is that none grow larger than 100-125mm (4-5in) and they are peaceful towards all other aquarium fishes, except rival *Ancistrus* species! It is best to keep a single pair of Bristle-nosed Catfishes and to avoid mixing them with other *Ancistrus* species in a small aquarium.

A closely allied form, *Peckoltia* (Clown Plec), is very popular with enthusiasts because of its bright striped and spotted patterns and

## Small non-predatory catfishes

**Callichthyidae**
(Dwarf Armoured Catfishes)
*Aspidoras*
*Brochis*
*Corydoras*

**Loricariidae**
(Suckermouth and Whiptail Catfishes)
*Ancistrus*
*Farlowella*
*Hypoptopoma*
*Otocinclus*
*Peckoltia*
*Rineloricaria*

**Aspredenidae**
(Banjo Catfishes)
*Agmus*
*Bunocephalus*

**Auchenipteridae**
(Driftwood Catfishes)
*Tatia*
*Trachelyichthys*

**Doradidae**
(Talking Catfishes)
*Amblydoras*
*Platydoras*

**Pimelodidae**
(Naked Catfishes)
*Brachyrhamdia*
*Microglanis*
*Pimelodella*

its small adult size. Smaller species of loricariids include *Otocinclus* (adult at 50mm/2in) and *Hypoptopoma* (adult at 100mm/4in). The Whiptail Catfishes (*Rineloricaria*) are not such keen algae eaters but they are attractively patterned with dark brown and sandy grey bands.

**Aspredenidae** Of the smaller unusual catfish species, the Banjo Catfishes, *Agmus* (Craggy Headed) and *Bunocephalus* (Bicoloured Banjo), often catch the eye of new fishkeepers. The term 'banjo' stems from the fishes' pan-shaped heads and long tails. These fishes will thrive in all sizes of aquarium, and are especially suited to the smaller community tank measuring 60x30x30cm (24x12x12in).

**Auchenipteridae** Other unusual catfishes suitable for the small to medium-sized community aquarium are *Tatia* and *Trachelyichthys*. These so-called Dwarf Driftwood Catfishes are adult at 50-75mm (2-3in) and so named because they resemble pieces of gnarled wood. Like the Banjo Catfishes, they are nocturnal, but this has never deterred fishkeepers who search for the new and unusual. The reason for their attraction often lies precisely in their shyness and secrecy; since they rarely venture out from hiding unless they are very hungry, an appearance is something of a novelty.

**Doradidae** The smaller doradids or Talking Catfishes, *Amblydoras* and *Platydoras*, are closely related to the Driftwood Catfishes and are often encountered by fishkeepers on the search for the weird and wonderful. Aquarium size is almost irrelevant; these 'badger fishes' like nothing better than hiding in a craggy hole in a piece of bogwood and remaining there until the room is quiet and dark.

**Pimelodidae** These Scaleless or Naked Catfishes are very active in the aquarium. As free-swimming

fishes, they require a little more space than some other species; ideally you should house them in an aquarium at least 90cm (36in) long. The smaller forms, *Brachyrhamdia*, *Microglanis* and *Pimelodella*, are predatory, but their modest size (50-100mm/ 2-4in) means that you can keep them in a community aquarium with all but the smallest fishes.

**Medium to large non-predatory catfishes**
Some fishkeepers will want to maintain a more impressively sized community aquarium. Keeping catfishes which scavenge for food rather than attack prey will enable you to fulfill such an ambition without having to worry about compatibility between catfishes and other groups of fishes. Here we review non-predatory species from 100mm (4in) to some huge loricariids at 600mm (24in).

**Callichthyidae** The lesser-known cousins of *Corydoras* – *Dianema*, *Hoplosternum*, and *Callichthys* – are larger, but equally peaceful. All are ideal for the large community aquarium (120cm/48in long) and are perfect as 'sweepers-up' of excess food. Although they will not withstand the aggressive attentions of African and Central American cichlids, you could include them in a community with South American cichlids (*Aequidens*, *Cichlasoma* and *Geophagus*) and larger tetras (*Metynnis*, *Myleus colossoma*, *Anostomus* and *Leporinus*, etc.).

**Loricariidae** The Common Plec (*Hypostomus plecostomus*) and related species, such as the larger Sailfin or Snow King Plec (*Pterygoplichthys*), are popular catfishes in this category. *Hypostomus* can grow to about 300mm (12in) in length, and *Pterygoplichthys* can reach lengths of about 600mm (24in).
  Certain larger loricariids, such as the Royal Plecs (*Panaque*), have special teeth to rasp at the vegetation. These catfishes are

## Medium to large non-predatory catfishes

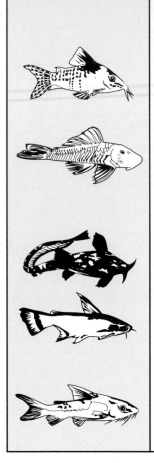

**Callichthyidae**
(Dwarf Armoured Catfishes)
*Callichthys*
*Dianema*
*Hoplosternum*

**Loricariidae**
(Suckermouth and Whiptail
Catfishes)
*Hypostomus plecostomus*
*Panaque nigrolineatus*
*Panaque suttoni*
*Pterygoplichthys*
*Sturisoma*

**Aspredenidae**
(Banjo Catfishes)
*Aspredo*

**Auchenipteridae**
(Driftwood Catfishes)
*Auchenipterichthys*
*Liosomadoras oncinus*
*Parauchenipterus*

**Doradidae**
(Talking Catfishes)
*Pseudodoras niger*

unusual in that *Panaque
nigrolineatus* has red eyes while
those of *Panaque suttoni* are a
vivid blue in colour.

Other large loricariid forms that
will grace any community include
*Sturisoma*, the Giant Whiptail or
Giant Twig Catfishes. These
popular and intriguing catfishes
have fin extensions almost as long
as their bodies, and sport
attractive brown and beige striped
patterns, even when fully grown at
200-300mm (8-12in). Although
these catfishes are often territorial
with their own kind, they are
peaceful with other species.

**Aspredenidae** Another group of
catfishes that are encountered less
often than the Common Plec are
the large Eel Banjo Catfishes (up to
300mm/12in long). *Aspredo
cotylephorus* (formerly *Platystacus*)
are found in and around river
estuaries, and are suited to large,
slightly salty water aquariums.
However, they will gradually adapt
to standard community water,
providing regular partial water
changes are made. These
catfishes are specialized
crustacean feeders, require bright
neutral water and will not thrive in
small overcrowded communities.

**Auchenipteridae** The larger Driftwood Catfishes are less widely seen in aquarium shops than other sizeable South American species. Catfishes in this category include *Parauchenipterus*, which will need an aquarium with a depth of at least 45cm (18in), and the regularly imported Peruvian Zamora catfish, *Auchenipterichthys thoracatus*. There is one rare species so brightly patterned that even non-catfish enthusiasts are attracted to it – the Jaguar Catfish (*Liosomadoras oncinus*) from Brazil – so named because of its feline striped patterns.

**Doradidae** The largest of the non-predatory catfishes belong to this Giant Talking Catfish family. The armoured or plated *Pseudodoras niger* can grow from only 75mm (3in) to 600mm (24in) in captivity if given enough space (i.e. a 450-litre/100-gallon aquarium).

**Predatory catfishes**
Predatory catfishes should be sold with a red warning sticker to alert the fishkeeper! However, they can often be identified by their possession of a forward-reaching mouth and long flowing barbels. There is a place for predatory species in communities that contain fishes which can fend off attackers or are physically too large to be consumed!

**Ariidae** The most widespread catfish family in the world includes only one species imported for aquariums: *Arius*, the Shark Catfish. This species is found in the sea mouths of major rivers in South America, Africa, Australia and in Asia (where it is known as *Trachysurus*), and will grow to between 300 and 600mm (12-24in) in length. It often comes as a surprise to catfish enthusiasts to discover that the 50mm (2in) young Colombian Shark Catfish, so distinctive with its beautiful silver body and brilliant white-tipped fins, will grow into this huge, grey catfish, capable of carrying over 100 small marble-sized eggs in its mouth. This is a catfish for the large, brackish water aquarium about 100-200cm (39-78in) long.

**Pimelodidae** These 'Sharks of the Amazon' – as the larger pimelodids are called – are very

**Predatory catfishes**

**Ariidae**
(Shark Catfishes)
*Arius seemani*

**Pimelodidae**
(Naked Catfishes)
*Leiarius*
*Perrunichthys*
*Phractocephalus hemioliopterus*
*Pimelodus blochi*
*Pimelodus maculatus*
*Pimelodus ornatus*
*Pimelodus pictus*
*Pseudopimelodus raninus*
*Pseudoplatystoma fasciatum*
*Sorubim lima*

exciting for the enthusiast who has a taste for large exotic species. One of the best-known aquarium catfishes in this category, however, is the relatively small (150mm/6in) Angelica or Polka-dot Catfish, *Pimelodus pictus*. There are several species of *Pimelodus*, including *Pimelodus blochi* (the most common species), *Pimelodus maculatus* (with a pattern to match the stunning Polka-dot Catfish), and *Pimelodus ornatus*, which can grow to 300mm (12in) and is suitable only for large aquariums.

One advantage of the common *Pimelodus* is that it is very robust and a suitable companion for large cichlids and tetras. Although large specimens will often consume small tetras in the community aquarium, well-fed *Pimelodus* tend to be lazy and less predatory. It is wise, nevertheless, to keep them only with fishes that they cannot fit into their open mouths; communities of larger barbs, tetras and gouramies would therefore be ideal. As free-swimmers, *Pimelodus* catfishes are best housed in an aquarium at least 90cm (36in) long, and they will thrive as a small shoal in an aquarium 120cm (48in) long. The depth of the tank is not as important; an ideal size is 120x38x30cm (48x15x12in).

*Pseudopimelodus* are giant *Microglanis*-like catfishes. They are secretive species and are best kept in well-planted aquariums at least 90cm (36in) in length.

In the large class, suitable only for aquariums 150cm (60in) long and reasonably wide and deep, there are some exciting species. These include the real 'pike-like' killers of the aquarium, such as the Sailfin Pim (*Leiarius pictus*) and Shovel-nosed Catfishes (*Sorubim lima*). One, the Red Tail Catfish (*Phractocephalus hemioliopterus*), is also known as the Emperor of the Amazon and, although best kept in large public aquariums, there is a trend in Europe, USA and Japan to keep such predators as individual pets. However, this catfish is strictly 'one to a tank' and should

## Catfishes in the community aquarium
Key
1 Pterophyllum scalare
2 Aequidens curviceps
3 Hyphessobrycon pulchripinnis
4 Carnegiella marthae
5 Hemigrammus ocellifer
6 Corydoras trilineatus
7 Corydoras aeneus
8 Peckoltia pulcher
9 Dianema longibarbis
10 Amblydoras hancocki
11 Otocinclus vestitus
12 Dianema urostriata
13 Rineloricaria lanceolata
14 Microglanis iheringi
15 Brachyrhamdia imitator

1 Chilodus punctatus
2 Carnegiella marthae
3 Paracheirodon innesi
4 Hemigrammus ocellifer
5 Nannostomus trifasciatus
6 Sturisoma aureum
7 Hypostomus plecostomus
8 Brochis splendens
9 Corydoras acutus
10 Corydoras barbatus
11 Corydoras paleatus
12 Farlowella gracilis
13 Bunocephalus amaurus

1 Myleus rubripinnis rubripinnis
2 Anostomus anostomus
3 Leporinus affinis
4 Pimelodus maculatus
5 Sorubim lima
6 Liosomadoras oncinus

Right: *Most catfishes will live peacefully with other fishes. In these suggested communities, catfishes are highlighted in blue.*

be kept in the largest aquarium that you can provide.

The Sailfin Catfishes, *Leiarius* and *Perrunichthys* (some confusion exists over the differentiation between these two closely related forms), attain lengths of 600mm (24in) and can be kept as solitary individuals in aquariums over 150cm (60in) long. The width and depth of the aquarium (each should not be less than 45-50cm/18-20in) are critical to the well-being of these larger

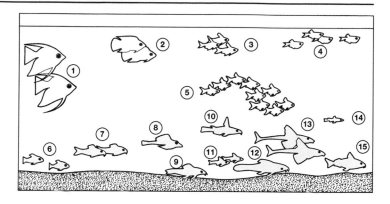

Above: *Non-predatory community*
Tank size: 90x38x30cm (36x15x12in)

Below: *Non-predatory community*
Tank size: 120x45x38cm (48x18x15in)

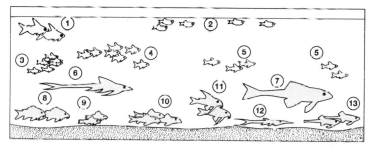

Below: *Predatory community. Tank size: 120x45x38cm (48x18x15in)*

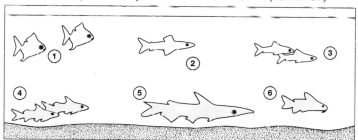

pimelodid species.

*Sorubim lima*, the common Shovel-nosed Catfish (450mm/18in), is virtually alone among larger catfishes in adapting successfully to restricted aquarium space. It can be kept in a tank 120cm (48in) long, but should really be offered more space as it reaches maturity.

*Pseudoplatystoma fasciatum*, the Tiger Catfish, requires a great deal of space if it is to grow to its full size. It is difficult to create a hard and fast rule, but generally you should allow a 300mm (12in) free-swimming catfish at least four to five times its own length in terms of aquarium space. The depth should be three times its length, and the width at least twice its length. In theory, a Tiger Catfish 600mm (24in) long should be kept in an aquarium 240cm (96in) long, 180cm (72in) deep and 120cm (48in) wide. In reality, the largest commercially available aquarium is likely to be somewhat smaller than

19

## A guide to stocking levels

### Non-predatory catfishes

| L×D×W | Capacity | Number of catfishes | |
| --- | --- | --- | --- |
| | | Up to 3in | 4 to 6in |
| 60×30×30cm (24×12×12in) | 54 litres (12 Imp./14 US galls) | 6-8 | 3 |
| 60×38×30cm (24×15×12in) | 68 litres (15 Imp./18 US galls) | 6-8 | 3 |
| 75×38×30cm (30×15×12in) | 85 litres (19 Imp./23 US galls) | 9-10 | 4 |
| 75×45×30cm (30×18×12in) | 101 litres (22 Imp./26 US galls) | 9-10 | 5 |
| 90×38×30cm (36×15×12in) | 103 litres (23 Imp./27 US galls) | 14-15 | 6 |
| 90×45×30cm (36×18×12in) | 121 litres (27 Imp./32 US galls) | 14-15 | 6 |
| 90×45×38cm (36×18×15in) | 154 litres (34 Imp./41 US galls) | 14-17 | 7 |
| 120×38×30cm (48×15×12in) | 137 litres (30 Imp./36 US galls) | 15-16 | 7 |
| 120×45×30cm (48×18×12in) | 162 litres (36 Imp./43 US galls) | 18-19 | 8 |
| 120×45×38cm (48×18×15in) | 205 litres (46 Imp./55 US galls) | 21-22 | 11 |

### Predatory catfishes

| L×D×W | Capacity | Number of catfishes | |
| --- | --- | --- | --- |
| | | Up to 10in | 10 to 36in |
| 120×45×30cm (48×18×12in) | 162 litres (36 Imp./43 US galls) | 2 | (1)* |
| 120×45×38cm (48×18×15in) | 205 litres (46 Imp./55 US galls) | 3 | (1)* |
| 150×45×38cm (60×18×15in) | 256 litres (57 Imp./68 US galls) | 4 | (1)* |
| 150×45×45cm (60×18×18in) | 304 litres (67 Imp./80 US galls) | 5 | (2)* |
| 180×45×45cm (72×18×18in) | 364 litres (81 Imp./97 US galls) | 6 | (2)* |
| 180×60×45cm (72×24×18in) | 486 litres (108 Imp./127 US galls) | 7 | (2)* |

*Sailfin or Tiger Catfishes, but *not* two of the same species

this, probably about 180cm (72in) long, 60cm (24in) deep and 60cm (24in) wide.

Large aquariums require extensive filters, several heater-thermostats and plenty of living space in the home. Most of the larger pimelodids are territorial by nature and will consume any other fishes that they can catch and hold between their jaws. You can lower the pH value of the water to subdue aggression; the more acidic the pH, the greater the carbon dioxide levels in the water and, therefore, the lower the oxygen level. You should then be able to keep certain territorial species together. Usually, however, peace is temporary and the smaller individual will be harrassed mercilessly through the dark hours.

### Siting the aquarium

Having decided on the catfishes you want to keep, and obtained the appropriate size of aquarium in which to accommodate them, you will need to find a suitable place to site the tank.

Catfishes are extremely sensitive to noise and vibrations. In common with other fishes, they possess a series of pores along the midline of the flanks – the so-called lateral line system – that react to vibrations in the water and transmit them directly to the nervous system. Catfishes also have a special link of tiny bones, or ossicles, that connect the inner ear to the front end of the swimbladder. In effect, the swimbladder acts like an 'ear drum', responding to sound waves and relaying the vibrations via the ossicles directly to the brain. These linking bones – known as the Weberian ossicles after their discoverer – also occur in knifefishes, carp, barbs, loaches and characins.

Catfishes may swim to the back of the aquarium on your approach, alerted by the sound of your footsteps. Wooden floorboards create a hollow noise that travels to the aquarium via metal stands, especially if the aquarium base is too close to the skirting boards. Placing an extra piece of carpet under the base should solve this problem. Although the fishes may become used to the sound of people passing, ideally you should place the aquarium in a quiet spot, and, since most catfishes are nocturnal, keep it away from very bright lighting and direct sunlight.

### How catfishes 'hear'

(A) Semicircular canals of the inner ear

(B) Fluid-filled sac that relays vibrations to the inner ear

(C) Weberian ossicles – a series of linking bones that transmit vibrations from the swimbladder to the inner ear

(D) Backbone

(E) Swimbladder – air-filled bladder that provides buoyancy, and also acts like a large 'ear drum', responding to sound waves and vibrations

# Water requirements and filtration

In this section, we look first at the natural water conditions in which catfishes thrive and then examine the factors that the fishkeeper can control in aiming to provide ideal conditions for catfishes in captivity.

**The catfish habitat**
In their natural South American habitat, catfishes are found at all stages of a river's development, from small brooks high in the mountains to the slow-moving waters of wide estuaries as the rivers pour out into the ocean.

Although the enclosed aquarium cannot exactly simulate the conditions found in the natural habitat, it is important to understand the natural water conditions so that as many factors as possible – water temperature, hardness, pH value and oxygen content – can be matched.

**In the mountains** the water is cool and fast flowing, often neutral to alkaline, slightly hard because of the high mineral content, and usually highly charged with oxygen. However, melting mountain snows can produce very acidic and very soft water. Sometimes these types of water mix to produce an average. The catfishes that live in these fast-flowing waters, such as *Chaetostoma* (the Bulldog Catfish), have smooth, flattened bodies, broad fins and wide, disc-shaped mouths to hold on to rocks and the river bed in the rapids.

Water movement in the aquarium to simulate these conditions can be achieved by using power head pumps driving undergravel filters, with internal power filters or, better still, by using external power filters with a venturi device in the aquarium return outlet that mixes air into the flow. The chemistry can be partly matched by mixing aerated rainwater (collected in a water barrel) with tapwater. Bulldog Catfishes can be kept with other catfishes in a community aquarium and these water conditions will often be equally acceptable to those species found in the lower reaches of the river.

**The forest rivers and creeks** are generally slower moving than the mountain springs (except in flood), and contain leaf and wood debris. Other loricariids are plentiful here, including the Common Plec (*Hypostomus*), Bristle-nosed Catfish (*Ancistrus*) and other small Suckermouths. Whiptail Catfishes (*Rineloricaria*) hide among pieces of submerged wood and groups of boulders, Twig Catfishes (*Farlowella*) lie camouflaged on branches in the marginal plants near the river banks, and small Suckermouths, *Otocinclus* and *Hypoptopoma*, can be seen in large shoals. *Corydoras* are as common here, in the shallow water, as they are at 3000m (9840ft) above sea level in the Andes and in the wide, slow rivers where they meet the sea. In the small creeks that meander through the forests, the Banjo Catfishes, *Bunocephalus* and *Agmus*, and the smaller doradids, *Amblydoras*, live in the leafy aquatic growths and on the sand banks.

The water quality in these areas will change with the wet and dry seasons, but on average the water is soft with a pH value of between 4.8 and 7.5, and temperatures of 22-35°C (72-95°F). A good average temperature for a South American catfish aquarium would be 28°C (82°F); any higher and the combination of low oxygen and low (acidic) pH will create breathing problems for the fishes.

**At the river mouth** all the above catfishes can be found, along with giant species, some of which, such as *Brachyplatystoma*, grow too big for even the largest aquarium. Giant doradids and sleek and streamlined pimelodids, such as the Tiger Catfish and the Red Tail Catfish, are at home in the wide and deep waters that flow in slow winding turns towards the ocean. Tidal influences mix sea water into the flowing fresh water at the mouth of the river, and this blend

can create an extreme range of water conditions, with currents frequently working against each other. It is virtually impossible to recreate the conditions that exist here at the end of a massive river's life, not least because of the sheer volume of water. However, if you do decide to keep these 'big cats', bright, neutral and fairly fresh water, which is well aerated and power filtered, will offer the best aquarium environment.

Above: *Large South American rivers, such as the Potaro (a tributary of the Essequibo in Guyana), shown here, contain many species of catfishes, but are dominated by giant predatory forms.*

Below: *Small backwater streams, such as the Compagnie creek in Surinam, shown here, are the nursery and protection waters for smaller catfish species, including the many forms of* Corydoras.

## Filtration in the aquarium

Much of our understanding of water chemistry in an enclosed aquarium system has come about in recent years. Most fishkeepers are now familiar with the process of biological filtration in which oxygen-fed (aerobic) nitrifying bacteria convert otherwise poisonous ammonia ($NH_3$/$NH_4^+$), created through the decomposition of fish wastes and other organic debris, into slightly less toxic but still dangerous nitrites ($NO_2^-$), and then into relatively harmless nitrates ($NO_3^-$). This useful biological process can occur in undergravel, power, foam or trickle filtration systems.

**Undergravel filters** An aquarium containing a layer of gravel substrate should employ an undergravel filtration system. This is recommended even if you are also using external or internal power filters. Catfishes will generally remain close to the substrate and are usually the first to be affected should stagnation occur. If there is no passage of water through the substrate then anaerobic bacteria, which live on the carbon dioxide/sulphur of stagnation, will pollute the tank and be a source of infections.

Undergravel filters are run by air pumps or quieter internal power pumps, so called 'power heads', which have been adapted to fit on the top of the undergravel uplift. These pumps suck water through the gravel from beneath the undergravel filter plate via the vertical uplift pipe and thus create a downward flow through the gravel that prevents stagnation.

**Power filters** External and internal power filters not only mechanically sieve out particles from the water but also support colonies of nitrifying bacteria. In external designs, the water is siphoned from the aquarium, passed through a series of filter media, and then pumped back into the tank. This type of filter also aerates the aquarium water.

## Biological filtration

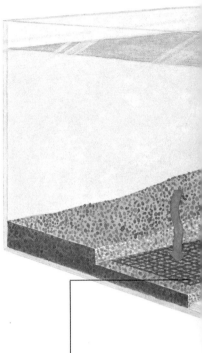

*A layer of nylon netting placed one or two centimetres above the undergravel filter plate will prevent this being exposed as the catfishes dig into the gravel. Cover the netting with at least 5cm (2in) of gravel and slope this upwards at the back of the tank.*

**Foam filters** These air-operated filters fit inside the aquarium and draw water through a foam cartridge. The foam traps particles mechanically and also supports the growth of nitrifying bacteria. Simple to install and maintain, these filters are available in a wide range of sizes; smaller models are especially suitable for breeding tanks because of their 'gentle'

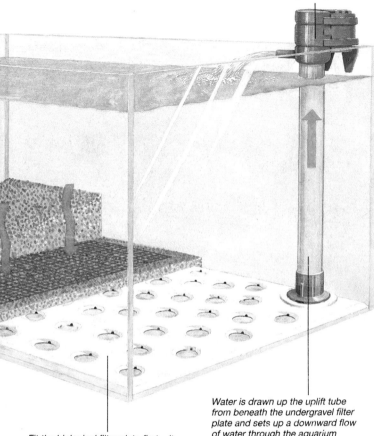

*An electric power head, fixed on the top of the uplift tube, speeds the water flow through the gravel.*

*Fit the biological filter plate first – it should cover the whole base of the aquarium to provide the greatest area for the bacterial colony to develop in the gravel.*

*Water is drawn up the uplift tube from beneath the undergravel filter plate and sets up a downward flow of water through the aquarium gravel. As well as allowing biological filtration to occur, this also prevents stagnation in the lower levels of the tank, where most catfishes live.*

filtration action. Maintenance consists simply of removing the cartridge every one or two weeks and rinsing it out in a separate container of tank water – at the same temperature.

**Trickle filters** Here, the nitrification process occurs in pots or trays of filter media above the aquarium water surface. Since the media are exposed to atmospheric air, these support a rich bacterial growth in highly oxygenated conditions.

Sophisticated 'management' systems not only filter the water efficiently but also control the balance of the aquarium pH, and oxygen and carbon dioxide levels, usually with a priority towards encouraging good plant growth.

## External power filter

*Clean water returns to the aquarium having passed through the filter.*

*Power supply*

*Filter wool, usually some form of man-made fibre, such as dacron or nylon, extracts any remaining fine particles. Do not use glass wool.*

*Gravel as used in the aquarium forms an ideal filter medium.*

*Hollow ceramic pieces allow water to pass through but trap larger particles and organic debris.*

*Water inlet from aquarium.*

*Use a nylon scourer at the base of the canister as an initial filter.*

## The new aquarium

The new aquarium needs a few weeks to settle down. Eventually, natural bacteria will develop in the water to convert the organic wastes of fishes into non-poisonous substances. Until then, chemical imbalances between ammonia and nitrite can develop which, at high levels, are poisonous to fishes; continuous exposure can prove fatal. New aquarium systems, less than six weeks from the day fishes were introduced, are thus especially prone to such chemical reactions because the necessary nitrifying bacteria are not established.

Preventing dangerous peaks of ammonia and nitrite in the new aquarium should not prove difficult if you follow these basic rules:

**1** 'Seed' the new filter medium with living nitrifying bacteria by transferring either unwashed filter material or up to 5kg (11lb) of gravel, plus a few litres of water, from an existing aquarium to the new tank.

**2** Wash the box or power filter in tank water *not* tapwater, as chlorine and other disinfectants in the tapwater will suppress the useful bacteria in the filter medium.

**3** Try to resist adding too many new fishes in the first few weeks, and give the aquarium time to settle down. Some cloudiness will occur, but only change water if the nitrite level becomes dangerously high i.e. beyond 25mg/litre (ppm). There are simple-to-use test kits available for measuring ammonia and nitrite levels.

**4** Do not overfeed fishes, as this causes water imbalances. Feed little and often; new fishes tend to be at the growing stage, when a more-or-less continual supply of food is essential.

**5** Do not change more than 50% of the aquarium water at any one time without adding a dechlorinating agent, and only make such massive changes if there is an emergency, i.e. leakage, introduced poison/ pollutant, or if the aquarium has to be moved to a new location.

## Basic water chemistry: pH and hardness

### The pH of water

The degree of acidity or alkalinity of water is expressed in terms of pH value, which literally means 'hydrogen power'. The scale is based inversely on the concentration of hydrogen ions in the water; the more hydrogen ions, the more acid the water and lower the pH value. The pH scale ranges from 0 (extremely acidic) to 14 (extremely alkaline), with a pH value of 7 as the neutral point.

### pH scale

| 0 | 1 | 2 | 3 | 4 | 5 | 6 | 7 | 8 | 9 | 10 | 11 | 12 | 13 | 14 |
|---|---|---|---|---|---|---|---|---|---|----|----|----|----|----|

extremely
acidic

neutral

extremely
alkaline

The scale is logarithmic, which means that a pH value of 8 represents a ten-fold decrease in the hydrogen ion concentration compared to a pH value of 7. An apparently small change in pH, from say 6 to 8, therefore represents a hundred-fold decrease in the hydrogen ion concentration, which can cause severe stress to many fishes. A number of different tests for measuring pH are available. These include paper strip indicators, liquid pH test kits and more sophisticated electronic pH meters.

### Water hardness

Water hardness is related to the amounts of dissolved salts present in the water. Two types of hardness are important to the fishkeeper; *total* or *general hardness* (or GH), which is related to the levels of calcium and magnesium in the water, and *carbonate hardness* (or KH), which is related to the amounts of carbonate/bicarbonate present. Water hardness is measured by several different scales, including degrees of German hardness (dH°). On this scale, water with a hardness value of 3°dH or less is termed 'soft' (i.e. low in dissolved salts) and water with a hardness value of over 25°dH is termed 'very hard' (i.e. rich in dissolved salts). An alternative scale is based on milligrams of calcium carbonate ($CaCO_3$) per litre of water. Again, test kits are available from aquarium dealers.

### Water hardness in comparative terms

| dH° | Mg/litre $CaCO_3$ | Considered as: |
|---|---|---|
| 3 | 0-50 | Soft |
| 3-6 | 50-100 | Moderately soft |
| 6-12 | 100-200 | Slightly hard |
| 12-18 | 200-300 | Moderately hard |
| 18-25 | 300-450 | Hard |
| Over 25 | Over 450 | Very hard |

# Lighting and heating

Catfishes are nocturnal; they are the 'owls' and 'bats' of rivers and lakes around the world. Strictly speaking, most catfishes do not need artificial lighting at all. As long as some natural daylight reaches the tank – directly or indirectly – this will be enough to simulate the day/night cycle that they experience in the wild. In a community aquarium containing a wide range of fishes, however, this regime is simply not acceptable – mainly to the fishkeeper, who wants to *see* the fishes in the evening and perhaps grow light-hungry aquatic plants. A compromise is necessary to provide lighting that will satisfy both opposing requirements.

**Lighting the aquarium**
In practice, the community aquarium is traditionally lit with fluorescent tubes installed in a hood over the tank. It is usual to install the largest tube that will physically fit inside the hood. Certainly, fluorescent tubes offer the best means of lighting an aquarium; they are 'cool', are efficient and cheap to run, and are available in a wide range of different 'colours' that produce slightly different spectrums of light. The very popular Grolux type is ideal for encouraging plant growth and its 'warm' tone enhances the colour of the fishes in the aquarium. Since it is noticeably dimmer than the whiter, 'cooler' 'daylight-type' tubes, it is a good choice for an aquarium containing catfishes and offers a fine compromise for smaller tanks – say up to 75cm (30in) long. In large aquariums there is more space to experiment with a combination of different fluorescent lights.

Mercury vapour spotlights are also recognized as 'cool' lights. They give off less heat than standard spotlights, are good for plants and can be controlled on a dimmer switch. Try experimenting with spotlights that can be dimmed and varying the length of lighting periods. A darkened area containing few plants, to one side

of the aquarium, will encourage catfishes to come out of hiding. Other than their relatively high price, the main disadvantage with all types of spotlight is that they rely on an open-top arrangement in the aquarium, which is not always practical.

When installing any type of lighting over an aquarium, be sure to use waterproof connectors and lamps specifically designed or adapted for use near water.

Above: *Areas of light and shade in the aquarium are visually effective and are important for catfishes.*

**Lighting breeding aquariums**
Artificial lighting is not recommended in the breeding aquarium, as strong light may inhibit the spawning process of certain catfishes. Natural light will be sufficient to trigger early dusk to dawn breeding. If plants are required in the breeding aquarium (some catfishes prefer to place eggs on plant leaves) then you can use potted plants and transfer them occasionally to a well-lit aquarium to prevent them fading.

In the wild, fry congregate in the warm shallows, where algae and plankton are richest. Spotlights encourage healthy algae growth and help to warm the surface of the water for young fishes.

**Heating the aquarium**
Although it is thought that catfishes will survive temperatures of 18-24°C (64-75°F), it is advisable

to maintain an average temperature of around 27-29°C (81-84°F) in the aquarium. At higher temperatures fishes are more active, feed more eagerly, and the efficiency of biological filtration is increased because bacteria are more active in these warmer conditions.

Modern combined heater-thermostats, with the switching in the top part of the tube and the element in the lower part, are ideal for catfish aquariums. Take care however, to guard the heater element from catfishes, as they tend to rest against the unit and suffer body burns. Loosely cover the element with a roll of gravel tidy (a sheet of plastic with small uniform holes that allow water, but not gravel, to pass through) and secure it in place at the top of the unit with a plastic cable tie.

An aquarium sited in a cool room will be affected by the ambient air temperature, which will certainly fall at night. If the room is very cold in the winter months, you may need to increase the wattage by 25% to cope with the heat loss. Continual fluctuations and falls in temperatures will most certainly encourage infections. In a warm centrally heated room this problem will rarely occur.

A small rise in temperature at certain times of year need not cause concern, as this will not affect the fishes. An approximate guide to the amount of heat needed is to allow 200 watts per 90 litres (20 gallons) of water. (See the table for recommended number and wattage of heaters for various sizes of aquarium).

There are now external power filters on the market with a heater coil incorporated into the pump head. The coil heats the water as it passes through the filter and is pumped back into the aquarium. These so-called 'thermofilters' are expensive but they do keep the heater element outside the aquarium, thereby protecting catfishes from possible injuries as well as freeing the aquascape of obtrusive equipment.

## Recommended heating systems

| Aquarium size Length×depth×width (cm/in) Capacity (Litres and Imp./US gallons) |
|---|
| 60×38×30cm (24×15×12in) 68 litres (15 Imp./18 US gallons) 1×200 watt heater-thermostat |
| 75×45×30cm (30×18×12in) 101 litres (22 Imp./26 US gallons) 1×200 watt heater-thermostat |
| 90×38×30cm (36×15×12in) 103 litres (23 Imp./27 US gallons) 1×200 watt heater-thermostat |
| 90×45×38cm (36×18×15in) 154 litres (34 Imp./41 US gallons) 1×200 watt + 1×100 watt heater-thermostats |
| 120×38×30cm (48×15×12in) 137 litres (30 Imp./36 US gallons) 1×200 watt + 1×100 watt heater-thermostats |
| 120×45×30cm (48×18×12in) 162 litres (36 Imp./43 US gallons) 1×200 watt + 1×150 watt heater-thermostats |
| 150×45×38cm (60×18×15in) 256 litres (57 Imp./68 US gallons) 3×200 watt heater-thermostats |
| 180×45×45cm (72×18×18in) 364 litres (81 Imp./97 US gallons) 4×200 watt heater-thermostats |

# Aquascaping

The planned layout of the aquarium can make a difference to its overall appearance and can help fishes to adapt to captivity. Aquascaping that imitates as nearly as possible the natural habitat of the fishes, together with good water chemistry and feeding, can ensure that, even in basic community set-ups, the fishes thrive rather than simply survive.

## The natural habitat

In the rivers, creeks and streams of South America, boulders, leaves and waterlogged bark litter the substrate, and vegetation and submerged branches break through the water surface. Sunlight filters through the open waters but the banks are in shade; it is here, in the shadows, that catfishes rest during the daylight hours. It would be difficult to recreate in an aquarium the shallows and depths, the temperatures and water flow of a South American river, particularly since these change with the seasons and are shaped by droughts and floods. Nevertheless, it is possible to use this natural scenario as a guide when planning the layout of the aquarium. Here, we look in turn at the important aspects of an aquarium aquascape, from the substrate to the water surface.

## The substrate

Aquarium gravel is the ideal substrate for freshwater tropical tanks. Gravel can vary in colour, size and mineral content depending on its origins; the best gravel for filtration consists of hard, rounded, beach-worn particles of 3mm (0.1in) diameter, as these allow easy passage of water through the filter bed. Coarse grade gravel with particles 12.5mm (0.5in) in diameter will allow larger uneaten food particles to become trapped within the filter bed, and this will lead to pollution. Very fine gravel, on the other hand, will pack down, thus starving the filter bed of essential oxygen and leading to stagnation. The rounded baked clay granules used for plant drainage have been used in the aquarium with some success but prove an expensive alternative to standard gravel.

Sand, although a natural substrate, has its problems: it packs down faster than gravel and subsequent stagnation is accelerated. A fine river sand can be used in an aquarium where the primary source of filtration is a large-capacity external power filter. It is possible to use sand as a biological filter providing that it is not too deep, 50mm (2in) at the most, and that it is raked loose on

a weekly basis to prevent settling and packing. Planting in sand proves difficult, as the roots, gripping the sand, cause it to pack, and this can lead to poor plant growth and filtration problems. Thus, although catfishes seem to show a preference for sand – their barbels, evolved as sensory organs, are ideal for raking into silt and mud in search of food – gravel is generally preferred as an aquarium substrate.

Above: *Rain forest streams, such as this, the Arima river in Trinidad, will provide you with plenty of ideas for creating a suitable aquascape in the home aquarium housing South American catfishes.*

Below: *The balance between rounded stones and plants in this aquascape is ideal. Select smooth, river- or sea-worn rocks, as some scaleless catfishes may injure themselves on rough stones.*

31

## Boulders and branches

Large boulders look impressive in an aquarium but they can create 'dead spots' in filter beds. Collect boulders from the beach or from the river bed – the best ones are smooth, rounded and water worn. These are good for scaleless species, such as *Pimelodus*, as the rounded edges cannot scratch the skin, and are ideal for catfishes that live in fast-flowing waters, such as *Chaetostoma*. The loss in water flow through the filter bed can be compensated for by the combined use of external power filters and undergravel filters. You can use aquarium silicone sealant to fix smaller rocks together if necessary, but avoid piling too many rocks on each other, as a collapse could damage the aquarium glass.

Place bogwood, beech or oak branches between the dark and light areas of the aquarium and watch how the catfishes move from one shelter to another. All fishes are nervous about open spaces and debris connecting these areas will help to allay their timidity. Although heavy pieces of bogwood tend to conceal fishes rather than provide cover, some of the doradids (Talking Catfishes) and auchenipterids (Driftwood Catfishes) show a preference for gnarled woods which have hiding places within them.

Break dead wood from the tree but make sure that you have correctly identified it, as some woods are poisonous. The best woods to use are beech and oak. The former is particularly good because it produces less tannic acid colouring in the water than most woods. Strip the wood of bark and soak the piece in warm water for about 24 hours, discarding the wood if any fungus has developed.

The middle and upper water areas are often left open for midwater shoaling fishes in a community aquarium. Place long twisted lengths of beechwood in the aquarium, or stand pieces of slate on end between the substrate and the water surface, to give depth to the aquarium and to provide something for the middle and upper water shoaling fishes to swim around.

## Suitable plants

Java Fern (*Microsorium pteropus*) is a beautiful green, thick-leaved plant that can be loosely attached to bogwood or rocks and is self propagating – juvenile plants grow from the parent leaf. Tough-leaved plants, *Cryptocoryne* and a 'hedge' of *Hygrophila*, can be used to conceal equipment such as internal power filters, undergravel

## Aquascaping the catfish aquarium

*You can prevent the aquarium looking cluttered and protect the catfishes by covering heaters, and other such equipment, with hollow pieces of simulated wood.*

Above: *A good aquascape for South American catfishes should not only please the eye – enhancing the overall appearance of the aquarium – but, more importantly, provide areas of protection and retreat.*

uplift pipes and heater-thermostats. Chosen dark areas, ideal for catfish aquariums, can be 'planted' with groups of the 'new-wave' realistic plastic plants.

### The water surface

If the aquarium is not of the usual closed canopy variety, then it is possible to allow large pieces of beechwood to protrude from the water. Soften bright tank lighting by allowing the light to diffuse through the leaves of floating plants such as Water Lettuce (*Pistia stratiotes*) and Butterfly Fern (*Salvinia auriculata*); these are ideal as they are not over fussy about pH value and water temperature. Water lettuce drops long roots that provide the upper areas with cover, and some midwater catfishes, such as *Corydoras hastatus* and *Corydoras pygmaeus*, seem to enjoy feeding from particles of food trapped in these trailing roots. Bubblenest breeders, *Callichthys* and *Hoplosternum*, may use fragments of these floating plants to build their nests. Other catfishes, such as *Agmus* and *Trachelyichthys*, prefer to hide among the plants in the upper levels.

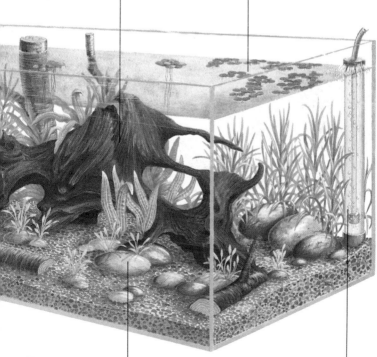

*Large twisted pieces of bogwood create perfect hideaways for catfishes. You should clean the wood thoroughly before introducing it into the aquarium.*

*There are many plants suitable for use in the aquarium. Floating plants provide welcome shade and many trail long roots that serve as cover for midwater swimmers.*

*Rocks should be smooth and rounded to protect fishes from injuries.*

*A 'hedge' of Hygrophila hides the undergravel uplift tube from view.*

33

# Feeding

The fishkeeper who first referred to catfishes as 'scavengers' may have known what the term really meant, but it has often been misunderstood since. Literally, 'scavengers' profit from the losers in the life and death struggle played out in nature. In practice, however, the so-called 'scavenging' catfishes are simply opportunists, making use of any food source they encounter. This might be ripe fruits and seeds that fall from trees along the river bank, a sudden 'bloom' of hatching insects, shrimps or crayfish, or the remains of a dead animal. In the dry season, when food is often in short supply, any food source is gratefully received, even by predatory fishes. At times, catfishes will live off the barest aquatic debris in the silt and mud.

In a carefully controlled community aquarium there may be little for the catfishes to scavenge – hardly any flake food, for example, may reach the substrate. Catfishes are not adverse to swimming to the surface to feed, but this is against their natural behaviour and is a sign of hunger or poor water quality. Most fishkeepers, however, are inclined to overfeed and you can, in any case, buy flake food in pellet form that will sink directly to the substrate, ensuring that catfishes in a community aquarium do not miss out at feeding times.

## Providing a balanced diet

The secret of good feeding is variation. Offer a correct balance of foods at frequent intervals – a little two or three times a day for small fishes. If you take care of the dietary requirements of your catfishes, your chances of running a healthy system are very high. A well-fed fish can withstand infection and cope with changes much better than a poorly fed one. Healthy fishes are also likely to reach sexual maturity much faster and to develop into good breeding stock (see *Breeding*, pages 44-49).

Here we examine the various food sources available for catfishes and how to prepare them, where necessary. In Part Two we identify the types of food required by each particular species (see pages 52 to 113).

## Manufactured and frozen foods

As mentioned above, there are several types of foods available that have been developed especially for catfishes. These include 'specialist' tablets, such as shrimp and gnat larvae, and others that are basically staple flake food compounded so that it falls in a lump to the substrate. Offer the fishes a good-quality staple flake

Below: *Catfishes sense food in the substrate with their barbels and then use their snouts to dig out morsels missed by other fishes.*

Above: *Many catfishes, including* Hypostomus *(shown here), will consume large quantities of greenfood such as lettuce.*

food in tablet form every other day and add shrimp and insect larvae, which form an important part of most catfishes' diets. There are some catfishes, notably doradids (or Talking Catfishes) and Driftwoods, that feed almost exclusively on invertebrates, supplementing this diet with seeds and fruits. 'Gamma' shrimp, widely available in frozen packets, is preferable to live freshwater shrimp, as the latter may introduce disease to the aquarium.

**Greenfoods**

Some catfishes, such as Whiptails, Bristle-nosed Catfishes (*Ancistrus*), and 'Plecs', require a high percentage of fibre and greenfood in their diet. Most fishes benefit from a regular supply of vegetable matter and, although they can be 'slow to catch on' when it is

introduced for the first time, almost all fishes will eventually relish 'greenfeeding'. Scalded lettuce, spinach leaf, peas and wild dandelion leaves are all ideal. It may be a good idea to ration flake food on the evening of feeding greenfood to give the fishes an appetite for this important part of their diet. Weight a whole lettuce in the centre with a stone and let the fishes pick at the leaf of their choice. Do not be afraid to offer large quantities of greenfood on a regular basis and allow it to remain in the aquarium for 48 hours so that it can soften naturally in the water. Remove stalks and uneaten pieces after this time to prevent water pollution.

Try supplementing these greenfoods with soft and ripe fruits, such as apples, pears, peaches and melons, which you should be able to buy cheaply at the end of the week in the supermarket. Allow these to remain in the aquarium no longer than a day, from dusk to dawn.

## Livefoods

The average garden can be a good source of livefood which, if carefully cleaned, you can offer to catfishes without fear of introducing disease. Compost, grass cuttings or potato peelings left in the garden are a perfect source of small red earthworms, which you can feed whole to larger fishes, including predatory species. Never collect worms from dubious sources, such as farm manure heaps, because of the high bacteria risk that accompanies them. It is a good idea, in any case, to clean earthworms before feeding them to the fishes. Place them in a container of damp grass or bran and keep them in a cool spot for two or three days. They will ingest the grass or bran and void their intestinal contents and they should then be safe for the fishes to consume.

Compost is also a source of whiteworm, which you can culture in a soil tray covered with glass. Fill it close to the top with slightly moistened peat and bury some bread soaked in milk just below the surface along with a small cluster of whiteworm. Replenish the bread at intervals and keep the peat moist and cool (around 20°C/68°F). After about a month you can start to remove whiteworms from the culture. Use tweezers to separate them, wash thoroughly and feed to the fishes.

Some catfishes, such as doradids, auchenipterids and pimelodids, will also eat flies and some smaller slugs, but you should avoid ladybirds and other beetles, and ants, because they can produce a nasty fluid.

Although it is possible to collect *Daphnia* (water fleas), bloodworm and *Tubifex* worms from local streams and ponds, it is much safer to obtain these livefoods from a dealer and/or known disease-free source. There is always the risk of introducing disease organisms – parasites, snails and leeches – with livefoods collected from the wild. A clean water butt in the garden, however, can be a useful source of fly larvae during the summer months and these will not introduce disease into the aquarium.

You can feed shrimp foods such as Mysis shrimp and brineshrimp (*Artemia salina*) providing you first rinse them of any excess salt under a warm tap. Larger shrimps, prawns and crayfish are also suitable, but soften them and break them up for smaller catfishes.

### Feeding predatory catfishes

Some of the larger predatory catfishes will accept foodsticks, pellets and large flakes as a staple part of their diet. Supplement these foods with large, cleaned earthworms. Fish predators, such as the Tiger and Red Tail Catfishes, will thrive on a diet of large earthworms, balanced with prawns and freshwater trout from the fish market. Avoid oily foods, however, such as whitebait and mackerel, since these can lead to regurgitation.

Large fishes will feed and then digest the food in their stomach acids over a period of several days. Do not feed them every day. In fact, some deliberate fasting is beneficial to the long-term health

Below: *A Red Tail Catfish will soon learn to feed out of your hand, but daily feeding of large predatory catfishes is not necessary.*

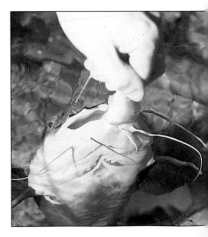

of large catfishes. It is difficult to resist the temptation to feed a catfish hovering at the water surface in a feeding stance. Red Tail, Tiger, and Shovel-nosed Catfishes, for example, are naturally greedy and will continually demand food once they recognize the hand that feeds them.

### Feeding new fishes

Always allow mature newcomers to the aquarium several days to settle before offering them food. Feeding should not be a priority with large catfishes, as they are used to feeding when food is plentiful and fasting during migration and the dry season. Large catfishes (60-90cm/24-36in) can take up to a month to settle into new surroundings. Sometimes, they will eat greedily and then regurgitate the food. This not only pollutes the water, but also overloads the filters, which may not have had time to 'mature'

in a biological sense in a newly set up aquarium.

Most aquarium fishes, however, are starved between capture and export, and are usually held in poor water conditions. Juvenile fishes, particularly, are likely to suffer from this treatment. Therefore feed young fishes as soon as possible, because their stomachs can dry up and contract, making feeding more difficult later on. Feed young fishes little and often until they are safely settled into the aquarium.

Finally, take care not to overfeed catfishes in a quarantine or breeding aquarium. It is much easier to feed a full community aquarium of fishes because the excess will be taken by the fishes that may have missed out initially. When there are only a few catfishes in a small aquarium, it is very easy to overfeed them. Measure the food carefully before introducing it into the aquarium.

### Livefoods in a water butt

*A clean water butt in the garden is ideal for culturing various livefoods suitable for catfishes.*

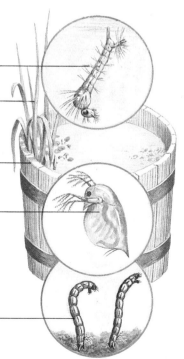

**Gnat larvae** *These wriggling foods will be relished by the fishes.*

**Plants** *You can add plants to the water butt, but make sure that they are from a disease-free source.*

**Container** *Make sure that the water container is clean and out of reach of frogs and other animals.*

**Water fleas** *These tiny crustaceans (Daphnia sp.) are ideal for feeding to catfishes, particularly to bring them into spawning condition.*

**Bloodworms** *These swimming larval stages in the life cycle of midges form a nutritious food for fishes.*

# Routine maintenance

Maintaining an established aquarium in a healthy condition should not prove difficult. Like weeding a garden, it is best to undertake routine maintenance tasks frequently. (A periodic large-scale spring clean will be beneficial to the health of the fishes and to the life of the aquarium as a whole, and we discuss this at the end of the section.)

## Water changes

You will need to establish a routine of making regular partial water changes – weekly, fortnightly or monthly, depending on stocking levels. Most aquariums are overstocked and therefore weekly partial water changes are necessary. (See page 40 for the special requirements of a breeding tank, where water changes are based on a pattern aimed at stimulating the fishes to spawn.) By changing part of the water, excess nitrates and organic waste products are removed and the balanced life of the enclosed system prolonged. A regular routine, a clean bucket, a siphon pipe/gravel cleaner and a water butt to store the fresh water will make the work much easier, especially if you have more than one aquarium to maintain.

Ideally, store water before the water change to allow time for chlorine to pass out of it, but if this is not possible then simply draw fresh water (adding some warm water to raise the temperature), stir vigorously and add a dechlorinator. Remove a set amount of water, usually 20-30%, from the aquarium using a gravel cleaner siphon set, and replace with fresh water. Be careful not to expose aquarium heaters; ideally, switch them off to prevent damage – but remember to switch them back on again! Only undertake larger water changes if the tank becomes polluted.

## Maintaining equipment

Rinse out power filter media in water that has been removed from the aquarium, *not* in tapwater. The efficiency of the filter media increases with age, so only throw away saturated filter floss or greased foam.

Clean external power filters only when the water flow return in the aquarium slows visibly to below 50% of the initial flow rate when the filter was installed. Again, you should wash out the contents in aquarium water (at the correct temperature and pH) so as not to destroy the essential bacteria, and then return them to the canister.

Clean the aquarium glass and remove any unsightly growth of algae on the front glass using a plastic scourer pad – do *not* use detergent! Ignore algae on rocks, bogwood and on the back of the aquarium glass, as it provides a natural source of pecking food for many fishes and helps to maintain a natural balance in the aquarium.

Check the filter pads in air pumps and replace them when they become clogged. Replace any airstones installed in the undergravel uplift tubes every two to three months.

Fluorescent tubes have a maximum lifespan of 18 months and should be replaced after that time. Even though they will continue to work beyond that period, the beneficial spectrum will have deteriorated.

## Spring cleaning the aquarium

Every community aquarium benefits from a spring clean every now and then, ideally twice a year, and you should plan this well in advance. About two days before the spring clean, store between 50 and 75% of the aquarium's water capacity in buckets or water butts (at room temperature if possible). Put down newspaper in front of the aquarium and remove all large rocks and bogwood. Give the gravel a vigorous stir, remove between 50 and 75% of the dirty water and replace with the stored fresh water. You should allow enough time for the filters to settle the water before you re-aquascape the aquarium. As a safety precaution, switch off the heaters and power filters before beginning the clean out. If the power is left on and they are exposed out of water, heaters will be damaged and the power filter inlets may run dry. Do not clean the power filter at this time as it is useful to have a mature filter working during a spring clean to cope with the extra fresh water input to the system. It is best not to feed the fishes for 24 hours before the planned clean out as they are likely to be shocked by the disturbance and create more waste. You will be surprised how quickly the fishes settle down and how clear the water appears after such a major spring clean.

| Maintaining an established aquarium | | | |
|---|---|---|---|
| | Daily | Weekly | Periodically |
| **Fishes** Check number and behaviour of fishes | ● | ● | ● |
| Feed fishes* | ● | | |
| **Water conditions** Partial water change | | ● | |
| Check temperature | ● | | |
| Measure pH and water hardness (at every water change) | | ● | |
| **Filters** Check filter flow | ● | | |
| Replace airstones in undergravel filter | | | ● |
| Check air supply carefully, clean air pump valves and filter | | | ● |
| **Plants** Remove dead leaves and excess sediment on leaves; thin out floating plants | | ● | |
| **General** Turn lights on/off | ● | | |
| Check electrical connections | | | ● |
| Renew fluorescent tubes | | | ● |
| Clean cover glass and remove algae from front glass of tank | | | ● |

*Some smaller fishes need feeding several times a day, larger fishes should be fed every few days.

# Health care

As always, prevention is better than a cure. Catfishes are hardy creatures and providing that you pay attention to water quality and filtration, and feed the fishes properly, you should not encounter many problems.

**New fishes**

Fish diseases are most likely to occur when fishes are first introduced to the aquarium or when they are stressed. Importers and vendors of tropical fishes cannot guarantee their health during collection and air freighting, when fishes are often crowded in poor conditions and fatalities are sometimes horrendous. The fishkeeper can unwittingly inherit most of the problems. A healthy catfish is generally quite resilient, but when it is stressed, underfed and has been in an overcrowded environment, disease can easily gain a foothold. Indeed, new fishes can be a 'time-bomb' of infections waiting to explode in an otherwise healthy aquarium.

Ideally, you should have a small quarantine aquarium in which to isolate and look after newly bought fishes. In reality, most new fishes are plunged straight into the aquarium, simply because they appeared healthy in the aquarium shop. If a new fish shows signs of infections when introduced to an established aquarium – itching, flicking, fast gill movements or lack of a healthy scale shine – then you should treat the whole aquarium and remove any severely infected fishes immediately to a separate aquarium to reduce the risk of a mass outbreak of disease. Even so, there is always a chance that parasite spores and/or bacteria will have already become established and begun to reproduce in the main aquarium.

**Problems in established tanks**

Health problems that occur in an established aquarium that cannot be traced to new introductions can have a variety of causes, including incorrect diet, poor water quality in the aquarium or overcrowding and bullying of the fishes. Sometimes disease can be introduced from an outside source, such as tapwater or stored rainwater, livefoods or unclean equipment. Let us consider these factors in turn.

You can easily improve the fishes' diet by feeding small frozen shrimp and insect larvae, lettuce, spinach leaves and a good flake food in rotation. Do not overfeed the fishes, however, but give them a little food at frequent intervals. It is a good idea to avoid feeding livefoods unless the fishes are isolated in a breeding aquarium and the food is essential to stimulate spawning. Livefoods, although nutritious, can spread infection by introducing disease organisms, leeches and snails into the aquarium, and these can be difficult to eradicate. Use suitable frozen foods instead; these carry no health risk and are as good as livefoods in nutritional terms.

If you suspect poor water conditions, first check the pH value of the aquarium water and if it is low (4.8-6.5) carry out a major water change as described on pages 38-39.

If the aquarium is overcrowded, either obtain another aquarium and divide the population between the two tanks, or thin out the stock and offer some to another fishkeeper or to the local aquarium shop (if possible, in return for food). Without doubt, overcrowding can cause disease and also makes it difficult to filter the aquarium properly. Watch out for the bully fish, or for possible indications of bullying, such as body damage. You can either remove the bully, or, if it is a favourite fish, transfer the fish or fishes that are being bullied to another aquarium.

Another possible route for disease is through equipment passed from one aquarium to another. It is essential to keep nets (used for transferring fishes) dry and clean after use. Some fishkeepers maintain that nets should be restricted to individual aquariums – a standard held by many major importers – to curb the spread of disease. Many outbreaks of disease in home aquariums undoubtedly could have been restricted to one tank had not nets, planting sticks, bogwood, plants, rocks and other aquarium equipment been transferred freely between the tanks.

### Treating disease

As we have seen, the critical first stage in coping with health problems that arise in the aquarium is to identify the cause. Clearly, if the problem stems from an environmental imbalance it is pointless, and possibly counter productive, to treat the resulting disease with appropriate remedies without first improving the conditions. Always look for the root cause of a problem and use remedies as the last resort.

Recognizing disease symptoms too late or applying the wrong treatment are all too common causes for fish losses. A common mistake is to confuse a parasitical infestation with a bacterial infection. A parasitical infestation will usually speckle the fins and increase the gill rate dramatically. A bacterial infection will manifest itself in symptoms such as missing scales, redness in the gills, fin damage or rot, and cloudy eyes.

If the fish is itching or breathing rapidly, then use an anti-parasite treatment. Do not be afraid of repeating doses after 48 hours, and remember to remove activated carbon from filters, since this may absorb some medications and thus reduce their effectiveness.

If slight fin or body damage has developed during the normal life of an aquarium, then use an anti-bacterial remedy over a period of several weeks until you see an improvement. In extreme cases of bacterial infection, such as dropsy (body swelling) and TB, you may need veterinary advice and the use of suitable antibiotics in a separate treatment tank. All too often, such infections arise from poor water quality and incorrect diet, often starting during capture and subsequent transport.

When treating fishes, always follow the recommendations given by the manufacturers of the remedy and allow time for the treatment to take effect; few remedies are instant. And remember: healthy aquarium conditions and a healthy diet make for healthy fishes.

*Below: The red areas on this fish are caused by a severe, and highly contagious bacterial infection which is difficult to treat without antibiotics (see table overleaf).*

## Table of health problems

| Symptoms | Possible causes | Action |
|---|---|---|
| Fishes flicking, itching and scraping body against gravel, wood or rockwork, increased gill rate | Parasite infection possibly introduced by new fishes | Use anti-parasite treatment. Doses can be repeated after 48 hours. Remove carbon from filters so that the effectiveness of the treatment is not impaired |
| | Incorrect pH, poor water quality, stagnant substrate, inadequate filtration | Carry out a partial water change and remove sediment from gravel. Check pH and add a pH corrector if necessary. Check filter and pump size to see if they are capable of coping with the system |
| | Excess ammonia/nitrite levels in a new aquarium | Carry out a partial water change and seed filter bed with mature gravel |
| | White spot (Ich) *(Ichthyophthirius multifiliis)* Freshwater velvet *(Oodinium pillularis)* | Use a proprietary white spot or velvet treatment |
| | Gill flukes *(Dactylogyrus* and other species) | Use a proprietary anti-parasite remedy |
| Speckled fins | Parasite infection | Use an anti-parasite treatment. Doses can be repeated after 48 hours. Remove carbon from filters so that the effectiveness of the treatment is not impaired |
| Fin damage/rot | Overcrowding | Check and revise stocking levels |
| | Bacterial infection | Use an antibacterial remedy |
| Fishes gasping at the water surface | Excess ammonia/nitrite levels in a new aquarium. Low oxygen | Carry out a partial water change and seed filter bed with mature gravel |
| | Incorrect pH, poor water quality, stagnant substrate, inadequate filtration | Carry out a partial water change and remove sediment from gravel. Check pH and add a pH corrector if necessary. Check filter and pump size |

| Symptoms | Possible causes | Action |
|----------|-----------------|--------|
| Bloated/swollen body | Incorrect diet | Check and revise feeding strategy |
| | TB (Mycobacterium) | Clean out the aquarium. Administer antibiotics in a quarantine tank |
| Cloudy eyes | Bacterial infection. Incorrect pH, poor water quality, stagnant substrate, inadequate filtration | Carry out a partial water change and remove sediment from gravel. Check pH and add a pH corrector if necessary. Check filter and pump size to see if they are capable of coping with the system. Add a general antibacterial treatment or tonic |
| Red blotches, gills inflamed | Gill flukes | Use a proprietary anti-parasite remedy |
| Fishes hanging in midwater in a vertical position | White spot (Ich) (Ichthyophthirius multifiliis) Freshwater velvet (Oodinium pillularis) | Use a proprietary white spot or velvet treatment as directed by the maker |
| | Excess ammonia/nitrite levels in a new aquarium | Carry out a partial water change and seed filter bed with mature gravel |
| | Incorrect pH, poor water quality, stagnant substrate, inadequate filtration | Carry out a partial water change and remove sediment from gravel. Check pH and add a pH corrector if necessary. Check filter and pump size to see if they are capable of coping with the system |
| | Water poisoned with insect spray, cleaning agents, etc. | Carry out a 100 percent water change. Use dechlorinating chemicals to avoid damage to filter beds |

# Breeding

Catfish breeding in aquariums was once restricted to two species of *Corydoras* (*aeneus* and *paleatus*), perhaps a single unidentified species of *Ancistrus* (Bristle-nosed Catfish), and sometimes, on very rare occasions, a *Rineloricaria* (Whiptail Catfish) species. Now it seems that, given the right conditions, most species can be bred in the aquarium. Success usually lies in the good mature condition of the fishes, a quiet aquarium, ideal water conditions, correct feeding and a good measure of patience!

Most wild fishes appear to know by instinct the correct time of year to spawn and this may be due to an ability to detect subtle pressure changes in the atmosphere. In the wild, catfishes spawn in the rainy season among the flooded grasses where there is plenty of fresh shallow water. Here the fry can grow up away from large predators. Before the rain storms, the air pressure fluctuates and the fishes congregate and become excited in the pre-spawning activity. For some catfishes, such as *Ancistrus* and *Rineloricaria*, these pressure changes act as a signal to seek out ideal spawning sites in submerged logs and in wood clusters.

## Spawning in the aquarium

It is advisable to establish a separate breeding aquarium for spawning all catfishes. Some catfishes require little inducement to spawn, others will not spawn without the 'trigger' of cool fresh water. To encourage the catfishes to spawn, you will need to recreate these changes that occur in the wild between dry and wet seasons.

To start the preparation sequence, increase the aquarium temperature by a few degrees every day. Providing the aquarium is open and there is good aeration from a power filter venturi and an air pump, you should be able to raise temperatures to 32°C/90°F. Keep water changes to a minimum for several months during the summer and then carry out a major

water change of about 75% using water at 18°C (64°F). This water will cool the aquarium, but providing all the occupants of your aquarium are well settled, you need not be afraid of the drop in temperature. This will recreate the rainy season influx of fresh, slightly cooler water, which is often the stimulus fishes need to spawn.

## The breeding aquarium

*Although many catfish species can be bred in the community aquarium, it is advisable to transfer them to a smaller, unlit aquarium to spawn.*

*Cover the heater-thermostat with a sheet of gravel tidy to protect the fishes from burns.*

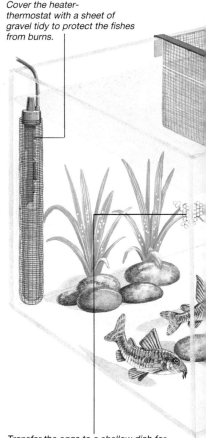

*Transfer the eggs to a shallow dish for hatching in fresh water. They will usually hatch within three to ten days and you can then move the young fishes to the fry net, hung in the breeding tank.*

Ideally, use water that has been stored and aerated for 24 hours to rid it of chlorine and other 'purification' chemicals. If much of the replacement water is fresh, then aerate it, warm it slightly (tapwater will be cooler than 18°C/64°F) and add a dechlorinator. At the same time give the power filter media a thorough clean in the old aquarium water. If you can collect rainwater, mix it 50-50 with tapwater during the water change.

It might be a good idea to increase feeding amounts or frequencies at this stage because the rainy season carries with it an abundance of fresh food and a general increase in the number of animals swept into the water.

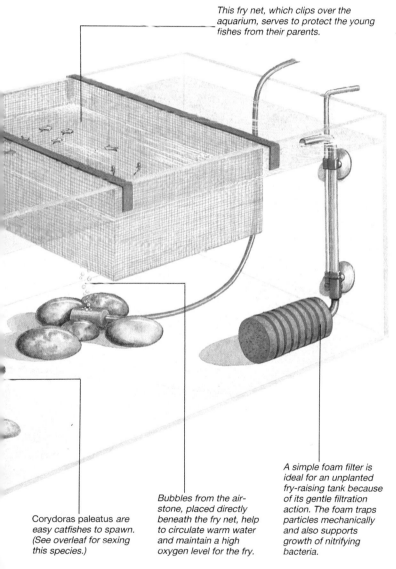

This fry net, which clips over the aquarium, serves to protect the young fishes from their parents.

Corydoras paleatus are easy catfishes to spawn. (See overleaf for sexing this species.)

Bubbles from the air-stone, placed directly beneath the fry net, help to circulate warm water and maintain a high oxygen level for the fry.

A simple foam filter is ideal for an unplanted fry-raising tank because of its gentle filtration action. The foam traps particles mechanically and also supports growth of nitrifying bacteria.

We will now look at how to breed specific groups of catfishes in the aquarium. Further advice on breeding individual species can be found in Part Two.

### Breeding in Callichthyidae (Dwarf Armoured Catfishes)

*Corydoras* are the easiest catfishes to spawn; almost 40 species have been spawned in the aquarium. *Corydoras* can be sexed by size and shape in maturity; males, for example, are noticeably more slender than females. Difficulty in sexing the fishes is an indication that they are not mature.

**Corydoras paleatus** *Male*

*Female*

Above: Corydoras, *and most other catfishes, can be sexed visually. The female* Corydoras paleatus *(bottom) is usually deeper-bodied.*

Transfer the breeding pair to a small unlit aquarium with a light scattering of sand or gravel, where they should oblige! Provide a potted plant, such as an Amazon sword, in the tank for species that lay their eggs on plant leaves.

Some species, such as *Corydoras pygmaeus* and *Corydoras elegans*, prefer to place eggs singly on the leaves of plants, while others, including *Corydoras barbatus*, lay them in distinctive groups of five or seven high up on the aquarium glass – equivalent to laying them high in flooded grasses in the wild. By contrast, some species, among them *Corydoras aeneus* and *Corydoras paleatus*, lay their eggs anywhere in a seemingly haphazard manner. Allow the eggs to remain in place for 24 hours and then remove them to a shallow dish for hatching in fresh (day-old) water, as the parents of all *Corydoras* species are likely to consume the eggs. Hatching times appear to be wholly dependent on water temperatures. The fry can be raised to the two-to-three-month stage in a net hung in the breeding aquarium (see pages 44-5 and 49).

Below: *Mature* Corydoras paleatus *spawn very easily in the aquarium and they are usually the first 'egglayer' success for fishkeepers.*

Brochis should be treated in the same manner as Corydoras, as the two genera spawn identically, although it appears to be more difficult to induce. Aspiduras lay up to 50 eggs, but hatchings are reported to be very poor.

Callichthys and Hoplosternum males construct a nest out of bubbles that they 'blow' and place on the water surface among any floating debris. Some fishkeepers float a plastic lid or polystyrene tile on the water surface; the fishes will invariably place their eggs on this 'nest' during the spawning twists that follow the fertilization 'clinches'. Eggs that fail to stay in the bubblenest will be recovered from the substrate by the fish and promptly replaced in the nest. You can remove both parents at this stage, although it is quite safe to leave the male in the tank; he will tend the nest until the eggs hatch after about seven days.

**Breeding in Loricariidae (Suckermouth and Whiptail Catfishes)**
There are often obvious differences between male and female Suckermouth Catfishes, the most noticeable being the prominent development of bristles on the cheeks of adult males during the breeding season. If you cannot see any bristles, try catching the fish in question and gently stroking the cheek.

Above: *This typical* Hoplosternum thoracatum *bubblenest has been created around leaf debris on the water surface of the stream.*

Unfortunately, this method of sexing is not totally reliable, since females can also have slight bristling on the head and cheeks.

Ancistrus spawn easily and the 50-75 fry can be raised in the community aquarium because, as with all loricariids, the male will protect them.

The close relatives of the Bristle-nosed Catfishes, Peckoltia (adult at 100-150mm/4-6in) are not so easily spawned in the aquarium. The ideal situation would be to have up to four females to the one male which would cut down the aggression against individuals. The male of the species will show protective parental care long after the fry have hatched.

Several species of Rineloricaria (adult at 150mm/6in) have been spawned successfully in the aquarium in a 50-75mm (2-3in) diameter PVC tube placed in the tank as a substitute for the hollow logs in which these fishes spawn in the wild. Males care for the eggs and then the 50-100 fry. Farlowella and Sturisoma spawn on aquarium glass and plant leaves and although the parents will tend to the eggs, the fry are best removed to shallow 50-75mm (2-3in) well-aerated water.

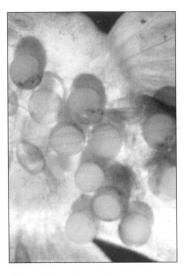

The smaller loricariids – *Otocinclus*, *Hypoptopoma* and *Parotocinclus* – have been spawned in the aquarium. They choose broad-leaved plants on which to place their eggs; unfortunately, hatching has generally proved difficult.

Male *Loricariichthys* have an enlarged mouth and lips in which they carry the eggs and fry. However, spawnings are extremely rare in aquariums because of the large adult size of these fishes.

*Hypostomus* (adult at 300mm/12in) and *Pterygoplichthys* (adult at 600mm/24in) are both spawned in the dirt ponds of Florida and Singapore, where they burrow in the soft soil banking and spawn inside the tunnels, but both species are too large to be spawned in the aquarium.

Above: *These* Aspredo *eggs are attached to the ventral area, thus allowing the fish to carry them in safety to fresh water to hatch.*

Below: *The burrows in this drained Florida pond provide spawning sites for* Hypostomus *(shown here) and* Pterygoplichthys.

### Breeding in other South American Catfishes

*Agamyxis* (Spotted Talking Catfishes) spawn in a nest among surface plants. Place a pair in a small well-planted aquarium and induce spawning with a partial

cold water change of up to 50%.

There have been isolated spawnings of auchenipterids (Driftwood Catfishes), but without fry raised. Almost all species are known to employ internal fertilization and the eggs are deposited several days later. Males generally possess adapted anal fin/genital extensions to facilitate copulation. Males and females chase and the two entwine during copulation.

*Bunocephalus* spawn in the substrate, laying eggs freely. The eggs should hatch in three days in soft, slightly acidic water at a temperature of 28°C (82°F).

The Eel Banjo Catfishes, *Aspredo*, carry eggs attached to the stomach; imported specimens seen to be carrying eggs have been isolated and the eggs successfully hatched.

Pimelodids remain a challenge; most, with the possible exception of some of the smaller forms, such as *Brachyrhamdia* and *Microglanis*, are too large and too territorial to spawn in the aquarium. The small to medium-sized pimelodids are egg scatterers, and should be spawned in much the same way as Asian barbs. Introduce the pair – the female noticeably plumper than the male – into cool fresh water at 18-21°C (64-70°F). Make sure the tank has a grill or a layer of marbles on the floor to protect the falling eggs from the parents.

The author has stripped milt from an adult pimelodid by stroking the fish in the genital region. If females could be stripped in this way, artificial fertilization might be possible.

**Caring for fry**

Although, of course, it is possible to leave the eggs and fry of many species in the community aquarium to 'take their chances', you can improve the egg hatching rate and the fry development of all species by providing a helpful hand. The easiest way is simply to remove the eggs from the leaf, wood, tube or aquarium glass and transfer them to a long aquarium with water only 50-100mm (2-4in) deep. Alternatively, hang a fry net in the breeding aquarium. This will provide the same shallow water but is less spacious. Hatching times vary depending on the temperature, but 3-10 days from the spawning day is the usual range. Once the fry have hatched and consumed their egg-sacs, provide strong spotlighting (using suitably waterproofed lamps) to warm the water surface and encourage the growth of algae.

In the wild, the fry swim to the warmer shallows, where there is an abundance of algae and other foods. As well as encouraging algal growth in the tank, also provide a constant supply of other greenfood (such as lightly boiled spinach and scalded lettuce) plus suitable fry flakes and freshly hatched brineshrimp (in very small quantities because of the salt). Keep pollution down by placing internal power filters on their sides in the shallow water.

| Typical feeding table for fry | |
| --- | --- |
| 48-72 hours | Infusoria |
| First week | Microworms, small amounts of brineshrimp |
| First month | Crumbled flake, scalded lettuce, small amounts of brineshrimp |

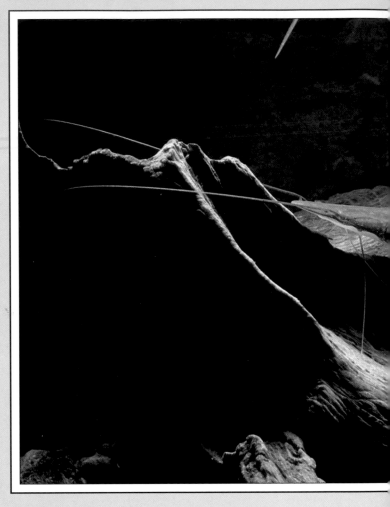

The variation of form and colour pattern of catfishes has long attracted enthusiasts and inspired them to learn more about one of the most incredible and adaptable of all fish groups in the world. The large number of species featured here, and their great diversity in terms of size, coloration and pattern, will soon dispel the myth of the dull, drab, ugly catfish living a nocturnal existence in the murky depths of a river or lake.

In this section, we examine over 90 species from the seven most well-known catfish families. Each group is introduced with details of characteristics and requirements typical of all, or most, of the fishes in the family. These groups, and the individual species within them, are listed alphabetically. The common names of species relate to the most popular usage, and specific habitat details are given where they are known. The sizes of the fishes are the lengths which they can attain in the aquarium and there may, therefore, be some discrepancy between these sizes

and other recorded scientific data. The latter may relate to individuals of no proven age (which may, therefore, be juveniles), the size the species can attain in the wild, or they may be simply the length of the largest specimen captured.

Needless to say, the fishkeeper will not be able to find all these species in the local aquarium shop. Some are very rare, and others are only encountered during certain seasons because catfishes are usually collected in the wild and imported.

An aquarium containing only catfishes, which are generally nocturnal, would be ghostly. However, the smaller species of this intriguing group of fishes are ideal for the community aquarium (see *Selecting catfishes for the aquarium*), where they live on the substrate, uninhabited by most other species. Larger individuals, some of which can grow as long as 600mm (24in), make striking inhabitants for the large aquarium (as single specimens or in groups of two or three) and provide a challenge for the enthusiast.

## Family: ARIIDAE Shark Catfishes

This family is spread across every tropical continent and species are found around coastlines and river estuaries. They are known as Shark Catfishes because of their erect fins and streamlined shape.

## Family: ASPREDENIDAE Banjo Catfishes

This family consists of two distinct groups: the larger 'eel' forms that live in estuaries and coastal swamps, and the smaller pan-shaped forms from slow-moving creeks. Aquarium breeding is not common, although there are accounts of spawnings of both groups in captivity.

# Agmus lyriformis

*Craggy Headed Banjo*
- **Habitat:** Leafy streams and creeks from Guyana to Brazil.
- **Length:** 75mm (3in).
- **Diet:** Insect larvae and invertebrates.
- **Sex differences:** Males are smaller and more colourful than females.
- **Aquarium breeding:** Not known.
- **Aquarium compatibility:** Will thrive in all sizes of tanks but is especially suited to the smaller community aquarium.

The pan-shaped heads and long tails give this group of catfishes their common name. The small Craggy Headed Banjo, with its distinctive ridges across the head, often catches the eye of new fishkeepers. It is widespread in Guyana and Brazil, where its dark and light brown patterns provide perfect camouflage as it lies motionless on the bed of slow-moving rivers.

Below: **Agmus lyriformis**
*This sleepy little catfish adds character to the aquarium.*

## Arius seemani
*Shark Catfish*
- **Habitat:** The mouths of river estuaries in the flow of the tide between fresh water and the sea.
- **Length:** 600mm (24in).
- **Diet:** Shrimps, crabs and fish.
- **Sex differences:** Males are more slender than females.
- **Aquarium breeding:** In the wild, the males are known to carry eggs and fry inside the mouth until they are able to fend for themselves. Spawning, which probably occurs in salt water, has never been recorded in an aquarium.
- **Aquarium compatibility:** Territorial among its own kind but reasonably peaceful with other fishes of equal size.

Left: **Arius seemani**

This brackish water Shark Catfish is imported from Colombia as a silver juvenile with black, white-edged fins and can grow from 50mm (2in) to 600mm (24in) if given the necessary aquarium space. Adult specimens can make loud croaking sounds by rotating the pectoral fin spine in its socket and transmitting the sound out of the swimbladder. This anti-predatory device is employed by a great number of catfishes. Like many catfishes, *Arius* produces a fluid in glands situated at the base of the pectoral spine, the poison reaching a would-be predator through the fish's sharp pectoral fin spines. Unlike other fishes, the Shark Catfish also has the ability to produce an anti-coagulant to increase bleeding in its prey.

## Aspredo cotylephorus
*Eel Banjo*
- **Habitat:** The brackish waters of the mangrove swamps in Venezuela, Guyana and Brazil.
- **Length:** 300mm (12in).
- **Diet:** Shrimps and other small crustaceans.
- **Sex differences:** Males are thought to be mottled in black, brown and white; females are relatively plain.
- **Aquarium breeding:** The author has successfully raised *Aspredo* fry in an aquarium from a specimen imported with eggs. The spawning and egg carrying functions have never been fully investigated and remain a mystery even to scientists currently researching the group. It is not certain how or where spawning occurs, nor when and how the eggs become attached to the stomach. It is thought to be the female which carries the eggs (attached to the stomach wall by miniature lengths of tissue, known as cotylephores or stalks) but sexing of this species (by colour patterning) is uncertain.
- **Aquarium compatibility:** A peaceful, non-predatory species. Will not thrive in small overcrowded communties.

Above: **Aspredo cotylephorus**
*The Eel Banjo, as intriguing as its relatives, is much the largest of the three species shown here. Give it plenty of swimming space.*

This catfish, formerly classified as *Platystacus*, but recently moved into the genus *Aspredo*, can grow up to 300mm (12in) long, although it is usually imported at 50-75mm (2-3in). It is common in the shoreline seas and river estuaries of northern South America and is best suited to bright, neutral-alkaline systems. It is known to migrate to fresh water and it is probable that the female carries eggs, attached to the stomach, to safer shallow water. Allow these fishes plenty of swimming space.

# Bunocephalus amaurus

*Bicoloured Banjo*
- **Habitat:** Slow-moving rivers and creeks.
- **Length:** 100-125mm (4-5in).
- **Diet:** Insect larvae and small invertebrates and crustaceans.
- **Sex differences:** Males are smaller and more slender than females.
- **Aquarium breeding:** Several eggs are laid freely on the substrate at night and should then be removed to a separate dish or net. Hatching occurs in three days.
- **Aquarium compatibility:** An excellent community catfish.

Right: **Bunocephalus amaurus**
*A great snail eater in the wild, the Bicoloured Banjo will relish small crustaceans in the aquarium.*

Almost every South American tropical fish import contains this species, which looks like a cross between a frying pan and a dead leaf! The Bicoloured Banjo will feign dead during the daytime but, like all nocturnal animals, it will come alive in the twilight hours.

---

Family: AUCHENIPTERIDAE Driftwood Catfishes

The Driftwoods, or Woodcats, are unusual scaleless catfishes and divide into estuary and creek forms. The brackish forms are fast swimmers and are usually streamlined in shape, whereas the inland water forms tend to be bulky. There are larger forms (*Parauchenipterus*) and pigmy forms (*Trachelyichthys*). Aquarium spawnings of all species are rare.

## Auchenipterichthys thoracatus

*Midnight Catfish*
- **Habitat:** Small inland rivers and creeks.
- **Length:** 100-125mm (4-5in).
- **Diet:** Insect larvae and small invertebrates and crustaceans.
- **Sex differences:** Males are more distinctively patterned than females with rows of white body dots, and they have an elongated tip to the anal fin which is used in spawning.
- **Aquarium breeding:** Fertilization is internal and the eggs are deposited to hatch within several days. No successful aquarium breeding has been recorded.
- **Aquarium compatibility:** Peaceful with fishes of equal size.

This small Driftwood catfish is regularly imported from the Peruvian Zamora region and can be distinguished by its rows of white specks on a dark blue body. As with all members of this family, it is extremely nocturnal.

## Entomocurus benjamini

*Winged Driftwood*
- **Habitat:** Bolivian rivers.
- **Length:** 75mm (3in).
- **Diet:** Small crustaceans and invertebrates.
- **Sex differences:** Males have distinctively long 'flying' pectorals and an extended anal fin.
- **Aquarium breeding:** Not known.
- **Aquarium compatibility:** Peaceful.

Although described in 1917, this catfish was virtually unknown among fishkeepers and scientists until 1985. It is similar to *Parauchenipterus* and could even be thought of as a pigmy variety of these species.

Above: **Entomocurus benjamini**
*This midwater swimming catfish
will tend to sulk on the substrate in
acidic water systems.*

Below:
**Auchenipterichthys thoracatus**
*This male Midnight Catfish
displays the extended anal fin.*

55

Right: **Liosomodoras oncinus**
*The Jaguar is quite shy but is a beautiful aquarium catfish.*

## Liosomadoras oncinus
*Jaguar Catfish*
● **Habitat**: Brazilian rivers and streams.
● **Length**: 150mm (6in).
● **Diet**: Small crustaceans, fish and assorted invertebrates.
● **Sex differences:** Males are more ornately patterned than females.
● **Aquarium breeding:** Not known, but the spawning method is presumably the same as for other Driftwood Catfishes.
● **Aquarium compatibility:** Fine with fishes of equal or greater size.

One of the most beautiful of all South American catfishes, the Jaguar Catfish can be recognized by the yellow blotches on a brown body. It is unique in that it possesses characteristics of two different catfish families. On the one hand, it is scaleless, as are all of the auchenipterids, while on the other, it possesses an outer gill spine and a long-based adipose fin, which are distinctive traits of the doradids, South American Talking or Thorny Catfishes. Scientists have argued as to which family it truly belongs, but current research places it in the *Auchenipteridae* family. From a fishkeeping point of view, the Jaguar Catfish has proved fairly easy to keep; it will accept a broad range of conditions and a wide variety of foods.

## Parauchenipterus galeatus
*Driftwood Catfish*
● **Habitat:** Almost all the main South American Amazonian rivers and creeks.
● **Length:** 200mm (8in).
● **Diet:** Small fish, crustaceans and assorted invertebrates.
● **Sex differences:** Males are more patterned than females, with the usual anal fin extension.
● **Aquarium breeding:** Although spawnings have not been recorded, the author has witnessed several breeding-like clinches of this species in which the male wraps its body into and around the female to copulate. Eggs are deposited some time

Below:
**Parauchenipterus galeatus**
*A good fish for the busy South American cichlid community.*

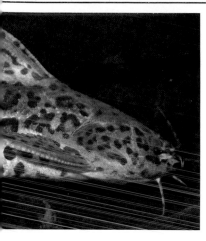

after spawning, so there is no immediate egg laying to confirm that spawning has taken place. It is possible that the eggs may be released at a much later date and promptly eaten by the parents or other fishes.
● **Aquarium compatibility:** Not suitable for the small community aquarium as it is predatory and will eat any fishes that are small enough to fit into its mouth.

This is the most common species recorded in South America. Males are more ornately patterned than females, with irregular black specks and lines on a beige body. Young specimens make interesting and unusual scavengers for the

modest-sized community aquarium (90-120cm/36-48in long). Mature adults, however, can be disruptive during the night time, digging up plants and chasing fishes out of caves, pots and bogwood hideaways, as they search for food and places in which they can conceal themselves during the day.

## Tatia aulopygia
*Black Pigmy Driftwood*
● **Habitat:** Small rivers and creeks.
● **Length:** 75mm (3in).
● **Diet:** Small invertebrates and crustaceans.
● **Sex differences:** Males have an extended anal fin.
● **Aquarium breeding:** Internal fertilization; eggs are deposited about 24-48 hours later.
● **Aquarium compatibility:** An ideal small community catfish.

This jet-black catfish has two colour forms, one plain black, the other speckled with white flecks. Both forms are sometimes imported from South America. These slender, torpedo-shaped catfishes live in and around submerged logs and riverbanks.

Below: **Tatia aulopygia**
*These delightful dwarf catfishes will thrive in the smallest community aquarium.*

## Trachelyichthys decaradiatus

*Guyanan Pigmy Driftwood*
● **Habitat:** Small creeks and rivulets of major rivers in Guyana and Brazil.
● **Length:** 75mm (3in).
● **Diet:** Small aquatic crustaceans and insects.
● **Sex differences:** Females are plain and slightly larger than males, which possess a modified anal fin used for copulation.
● **Aquarium breeding:** Eggs are fertilized internally, but it is not clear when they are discharged after copulation. Reports suggest scatterings of 40mm eggs; large in comparison with adult size.
● **Aquarium compatibility:** An ideal oddity for a compact aquarium but may predate on small fry.

This species has been known to science only since 1974. It was the only form known until a Peruvian species, *Trachelyichthys exilis*, was described in 1977. Imports are not common, although in recent years several specimens have found their way into shops.

Above:
**Trachelyichthys decaradiatus**
*Although rarely available, this small species is much sought after.*

## Trachelyopterichthys taeniatus

*Eel Driftwood*
● **Habitat:** Brazilian creeks and rivers, in and around submerged logs and forest litter.
● **Length:** 300mm (12in).
● **Diet:** Aquatic invertebrates, crustaceans and small fish fry.
● **Sex differences:** Males are much more brightly patterned and streamlined in body shape than their female counterparts.

● **Aquarium breeding:** Not known. Eggs are fertilized internally.
● **Aquarium compatibility:** Not recommended for community aquariums containing small livebearing fishes, tetras and rasboras, since the Eel Driftwood is likely to eat them in the twilight hours, when community fishes are inactive and nocturnal fishes are on the prowl!

This long, slender, yellow and brown striped catfish has been known to science for well over 120 years, but only became available to fishkeepers in 1983. A few specimens have been imported in recent years and have thrived in larger cichlid/catfish community aquariums. Adult Eel Driftwood Catfishes require a lot of swimming space and should not be kept in aquariums less than 150cm (60in) long. They show a preference for slightly acidic systems but can be gradually acclimatized to thrive at more neutral pH levels.

Family: CALLICHTHYIDAE Dwarf Armoured Catfishes

Known collectively as the Armoured Catfishes – a reference to the two rows of scutes or bony platelets which flank the body – these are undoubtedly the most popular catfishes available to fishkeepers. The *Corydoras* genus offers a great number of small species; other genera, such as *Callichthys*, *Dianema* and *Hoplosternum*, contain only a handful of species. All are ideal community aquarium fishes, although larger species may dig up plants in a small system. Most forms have been spawned in the aquarium, the main exception being *Dianema*. The smaller forms are egg layers, the larger forms are bubblenest breeders.

## Aspidoras albater
*False Macropterus*
● **Habitat:** Small Brazilian rivers.
● **Length:** 50mm (2in).
● **Diet:** Small insects and invertebrates.
● **Sex differences:** Males are more slender than females.
● **Aquarium breeding:** Not known, but almost certainly as for *Corydoras*.
● **Aquarium compatibility:** Peaceful.

Although quite rare, *Aspidoras albater* has been imported and sold as *Corydoras macropterus*. This close relative of the *Corydoras* has the same base brown colour and diagonal dark brown bars. *Aspidoras* have been found to be quite delicate on introduction to the aquarium and a high loss rate is reported by fishkeepers. Despite this, they appear to adapt well to a wide variety of water conditions once established. There are less than 20 species of *Aspidoras* known, of which only three or four have been kept by catfish enthusiasts.

Identification of individual species is very difficult and *Aspidoras pauciradiatus* is the only species whose identity has been clearly established.

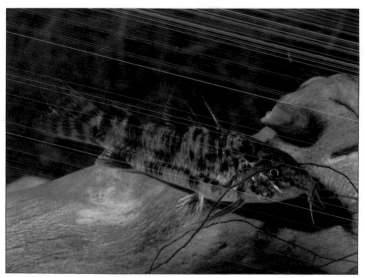

Left:
**Trachelyopterichthys taeniatus**
*The elongated body of the Eel Driftwood reveals its midwater swimming habits.*

Above: **Aspidoras albater**
*This species is often sold as* Corydoras macropterus. *Its small size and long head help distinguish it from the latter.*

# Aspidoras pauciradiatus
*False Corydoras*
- **Habitat:** Southern Brazil.
- **Length:** 25mm (1in).
- **Diet:** Very small invertebrates.
- **Sex differences:** Males are more slender than females.
- **Aquarium breeding:** Eggs are placed at random and can be difficult to hatch.
- **Aquarium compatibility:** Peaceful.

This commonly imported catfish is the best-known *Aspidoras* species and also one of the smallest. It was originally described in 1970 as a *Corydoras* because of its body shape, but can be distinguished by its long head. Its requirements are similar to those of *Corydoras* except that it can be more delicate on introduction to the aquarium. These fishes may rest motionless on the substrate and refuse to feed if confronted with adverse water conditions, such as low pH and poor filtration.

Above: **Aspidoras pauciradiatus**
*A superb miniature species for the small aquarium, this catfish seems fairly hardy once it has settled in the aquarium and is feeding.*

Below: **Brochis britskii**
*This catfish prefers deeper water and thrives on a shredded shrimp and insect larvae diet.*

# Brochis britskii
*Britski's Catfish*
- **Habitat:** Weed-choked slow rivers in the Mato Grosso region of Brazil.
- **Length:** 100mm (4in).
- **Diet:** Insect larvae and assorted crustaceans.
- **Sex differences:** Females are larger than males.
- **Aquarium breeding:** Not recorded, but probably as for *Corydoras*.
- **Aquarium compatibility:** Peaceful.

This superb Brazilian species has the emerald green *Brochis* sheen enhanced by a reddened hue in the caudal fin. It is very similar in appearance to *B. multiradiatus* from Ecuador and Peru, but lacks the latter's long snout.

*Brochis britskii* have been collected in the Rio Guapore in the Brazilian Mato Grosso region. They live in slow-moving, heavily planted rivers (3-6m/10-20ft deep), where the water is soft and has a pH of around 6.9-7.2.

Above: **Brochis splendens**
*Now a firm favourite, this robust species is an ideal addition to the community aquarium.*

# Brochis splendens
*Emerald Catfish*
● **Habitat:** Rivers in Peru, Ecuador and Brazil.
● **Length:** 75-100mm (3-4in).
● **Diet:** Small insect larvae and assorted invertebrates.
● **Sex differences:** Females are larger than males.
● **Aquarium breeding:** Egg layer as *Corydoras*.
● **Aquarium compatibility:** Peaceful.

Species in the *Brochis* genus can be distinguished from *Corydoras* by the presence of more dorsal rays. The Emerald Catfish, sometimes mistakenly known as *Brochis coeruleus*, is the most commonly imported species of the three described here. *Brochis* show a preference for deep aquariums (45-60cm/18-24in in depth) and are more active when kept in groups of between four and six specimens. They delve into the substrate for food more than most species of *Corydoras* and will also eat small shredded prawns and chopped earthworms.

61

# Brochis multiradiatus

*Hognosed Brochis*
- **Habitat:** Small rivers in Ecuador, Brazil and Peru.
- **Length:** 100-125mm (4-5in).
- **Diet:** Insect larvae and assorted crustaceans.
- **Sex differences:** Females are larger than males.
- **Aquarium breeding:** Not recorded but most probably as for *Corydoras*.
- **Aquarium compatibility:** Peaceful.

First discovered in Ecuador, this long-nosed, large-dorsal-rayed species has more recently been imported from Peru. It is considered to be one of the most beautiful of the smaller catfishes.

The long head and snout length of the Hognosed Brochis enable it to dig into the substrate in search of food, especially live bloodworm and *Tubifex*, which may have been missed by other fishes. They thrive in bright, neutral water.

Right: **Brochis multiradiatus**
*The rarest of these three* Brochis *species, the Hognosed form is happiest in a neutral to alkaline system with non-aggressive fishes.*

# Callichthys callichthys

*Armoured Catfish*
- **Habitat:** Tidal rivers in Guyana.
- **Length:** 180mm (7in).
- **Diet:** Shrimps and various small crustaceans.
- **Sex differences:** Males have thickened pectoral spines in maturity.
- **Aquarium breeding:** Males produce a bubblenest in much the same way as *Betta splendens* (Asian Fighting Fishes). The fertilized eggs are placed in the nest and guarded by the male.
- **Aquarium compatibility:** Peaceful, but prove greedy competitors for food.

*Callichthys* is often confused with *Hoplosternum* but can be distinguished by its flattened head, small eyes and rounded caudal fin. South American imports can sometimes prove difficult to keep and this is probably due to the overcrowded and inadequate conditions under which they are held before they are exported. They require a neutral water condition with a handful of aquarium salts.

Aquarium-raised specimens prove very adaptable and will thrive in a wide variety of conditions, accepting all prepared and fresh foods.

Right: **Callichthys callichthys**
*The smaller eyes of this catfish distinguish it from* Hoplosternum *with which it is often confused.*

# Corydoras acutus

*Black Top Catfish*
- **Habitat:** Peruvian rivers.
- **Length:** 75mm (3in).
- **Diet:** Insect larvae, aquatic worms and most small crustaceans and invertebrates.
- **Sex differences:** Males are more slender than females.
- **Aquarium breeding:** Egg laying among plants.
- **Aquarium compatibility:** Peaceful.

The Black Top is one of the snouted species of *Corydoras* that arrive in shipments along with the very popular *C. julii* catfishes. The Black Top Catfish has a long snout which it uses to dig into the substrate, sifting the gravel for food that other fishes may have missed. It shares the black dorsal spot with *Corydoras julii* and, when juveniles are mixed, it can sometimes be difficult to distinguish the two species. Like many of the Peruvian species, it seems to prefer bright, neutral waters, and will thrive in a properly maintained aquarium.

Right: **Corydoras acutus**
*A robust and peaceful species.*

## Corydoras adolfoi

*Adolf's Catfish*
● **Habitat:** Clear water offshoots of the Rio Negro in Brazil.
● **Length:** 50mm (2in).
● **Diet:** Insect larvae, aquatic worms and most small crustaceans and invertebrates.
● **Sex differences:** Females are slightly more robust in shape when carrying eggs.
● **Aquarium breeding:** Indiscriminate egg laying.
● **Aquarium compatibility:** Peaceful.

One of the most beautiful species of *Corydoras*, Adolf's Catfish is distinguished by its orange patch and high price! Discovered recently in the whitewater offshoots of the blackwater Rio Negro, it lives alongside its mimic, *Corydoras imitator*.

## Corydoras aeneus

*Bronze Catfish*
● **Habitat:** Widespread in South American rivers.
● **Length:** 75mm (3in).
● **Diet:** Insect larvae, aquatic worms and most small crustaceans and invertebrates.
● **Sex differences:** Females are larger than males.
● **Aquarium breeding:** Egg laying. Offspring are easily spawned and raised in aquariums.
● **Aquarium compatibility:** Peaceful.

Above: **Corydoras adolfoi**
*This attractive species requires bright neutral water conditions and will thrive when offered a shaded aquarium and a regular supply of finely shredded shrimp.*

The Bronze Catfish, so named because of the red-brown caste, is available in natural and albino forms. It is widespread across South America, from Trinidad to the coastline rivers of southern Brazil, and has long been farm raised and sold on the aquarium market. There are several wild forms, including a distinctive variety with a gold-flecked head, sometimes referred to as *Corydoras aeneus schultzi*.

Above: **Corydoras ambiacus**
*A robust and adaptable species, ideal for the community aquarium.*

Below: **Corydoras aeneus**
*The toughest and most easily bred of all South American catfishes.*

## Corydoras ambiacus
*Spotted Catfish*
● **Habitat:** Peruvian and Colombian rivers.
● **Length:** 75mm (3in).
● **Diet:** Insect larvae, aquatic worms and most small crustaceans and invertebrates.
● **Sex differences:** Females are larger than males.
● **Aquarium breeding:** One of the few species of *Corydoras* not yet spawned in the aquarium.
● **Aquarium compatibility:** Peaceful.

This species is well known to fishkeepers, although the scientific name is not commonly used. Although plentiful in the wild, and commonly imported, the Spotted Catfish has not been spawned in the aquarium. It is not generally fussy about its water conditions, but the key to breeding may well prove to be the provision of clear, neutral water.

# Corydoras arcuatus
*Skunk Catfish*
● **Habitat:** Peruvian and Brazilian rivers.
● **Length:** 50mm (2in).
● **Diet:** Insect larvae, aquatic worms and most small crustaceans and invertebrates.
● **Sex differences:** Females are slightly larger and deeper bodied than males.
● **Aquarium breeding:** About 20-30 eggs are laid among plants.
● **Aquarium compatibility:** Peaceful.

The Skunk Catfish, also known as the Bowline Catfish, has a distinctive, black upper body stripe that passes through the eye. This strong pattern provides camouflage to disguise it from aquatic and terrestial predators in the clear waters – from above the fish resembles a piece of debris. In the aquarium the Skunk Catfish will thrive in water that is neutral to slightly alkaline in pH value.

Below: **Corydoras arcuatus**
*Good filtration will alleviate risk of infection which can result in barbel loss in this species.*

Right: **Corydoras barbatus**
*The Bearded Catfish thrives in a broad range of water conditions and is suited to large communities.*

# Corydoras barbatus
*Bearded Catfish*
● **Habitat:** The coastal creeks of Brazil.
● **Length:** 100mm (4in).
● **Diet:** Insect larvae, aquatic worms and most small crustaceans and invertebrates.
● **Sex differences:** Males are slender and more distinctive in colour than females. In breeding condition, the males display head bristles.
● **Aquarium breeding:** Eggs are placed high on the aquarium glass in groups of five and seven.
● **Aquarium compatibility:** Peaceful.

One of the largest *Corydoras* catfishes. The male of this southern Brazilian species is one of a handful of species that develop cheek bristles in breeding condition. These catfishes will live comfortably in a wide range of water conditions and are easy to spawn in the aquarium.

## Corydoras bondi
*Bond's Catfish*
- **Habitat:** Venezuelan rivers.
- **Length:** 50mm (2in).
- **Diet:** Insect larvae, aquatic worms and most small crustaceans and invertebrates.
- **Sex differences:** Males are more slender than females.
- **Aquarium breeding:** Egg laying.
- **Aquarium compatibility:** Peaceful.

*Corydoras bondi* is found in another form known as *Corydoras bondi coppenamensis* from the Coppename River in Surinam. *Corydoras bondi bondi*, is a small pale tan catfish with a black mid lateral stripe and spots across the body. *Corydoras bondi coppenamensis* has a similar pattern but the head spots are larger and more clearly defined.

Bond's Catfish is easy to look after and will accept a broad range of water conditions.

Below: **Corydoras bondi**
*This peaceful little catfish will live most happily in the small community aquarium.*

## Corydoras delphax

*False Blochi Catfish*

- **Habitat:** Colombian rivers.
- **Length:** 75mm (3in).
- **Diet:** Insect larvae, aquatic worms and most small crustaceans and invertebrates.
- **Sex differences:** Males are smaller than females.
- **Aquarium breeding:** Egg laying as with other *Corydoras* species, but rarely spawned in an aquarium.
- **Aquarium compatibility:** Peaceful.

Below: **Corydoras delphax**
*A fast water species, the False Blochi Catfish is happiest in a large community aquarium.*

This Colombian species was originally incorrectly identified as *Corydoras blochi*. Although it has been known to aquarists for a long time, it was not scientifically described until 1983. It is one of the most frequently imported species and is a mainstay of Colombian tropical fish exports. It has proved to be very hardy and adaptable and is an ideal species for the non-predatory community aquarium. A range of colour forms exist. One is dark, almost black, and speckled with a pale saddle patch from the dorsal to the middle body region. Another form, which also has a saddle patch, is without the speckled pattern.

## Corydoras elegans

*Elegant Catfish*

- **Habitat:** Creeks and small rivers of Peru, Brazil and Ecuador.
- **Length:** 50mm (2in).
- **Diet:** Insect larvae, aquatic worms and most small crustaceans and invertebrates.
- **Sex differences:** Males are more highly patterned than ~~males.~~
- ~~Aq~~uarium breeding: Very easily ~~spaw~~ned when mature and the ~~y a~~re fairly robust, with very ~~hat~~ching rates.
- ~~Aquar~~ium compatibility:

This species is quite widespread in South America, although the majority of imported specimens are from Peru.

*Corydoras elegans* has generally proved extremely adaptable to a wide range of water conditions and is an excellent choice for the smaller community system.

Right: **Corydoras elegans**
*This small catfish is distinctive as one of only a handful of species in which males are more ornately patterned than females. This species is easy to sex and breeding successes are common.*

# Corydoras habrosus
*Salt and Pepper Catfish*
● **Habitat:** Colombian and Venezuelan rivers.
● **Length:** 25mm (1in).
● **Diet:** Insect larvae, aquatic worms and most small crustaceans and invertebrates.
● **Sex differences:** Females are slightly larger than males.
● **Aquarium breeding:** Will spawn in planted aquariums.
● **Aquarium compatibility:** Peaceful.

Above: **Corydoras habrosus**
*These pigmy catfishes are best kept in groups of six or more; they are happiest and most active when shoaling together.*

This tiny Venezuelan catfish (adult at 25mm/1in) is one of the smallest species in the genus. It is known in Colombia as *Corydoras cochui* (a valid Brazilian species according to current research) and this has caused much confusion in fishkeeping circles.

## Corydoras hastatus
*Tail Spot Pigmy Catfish*
● **Habitat:** Brazilian and Paraguayan rivers, in bright water.
● **Length:** 25mm (1in).
● **Diet:** Small aquatic invertebrates and algae.
● **Sex differences:** Males are smaller than females.
● **Aquarium breeding:** Considering their small adult size, these catfishes produce a few surprisingly large eggs. Some eggs will hatch in a well-planted aquarium, but many fishkeepers report that the adults eat the fry.
● **Aquarium compatibility:** Superb for the smallest community aquarium, but do not keep them in an aquarium containing larger cichlids or tetras; they are likely to be eaten!

Scientists once considered that the Paraguayan form differed from the Brazilian and another name – *Corydoras australe* – was used to identify the former. The black tail spot distinguishes this species from the Pigmy Catfish, *Corydoras pygmaeus*, which shares its diminutive size but also has a black lateral stripe as a further differentiating feature.

Below: **Corydoras hastatus**
*Another tiny species that thrives in shoals, Tail Spot Pigmy Catfishes are a delight to keep.*

## Corydoras julii
*Julii Catfish*
● **Habitat:** Brazilian rivers.
● **Length:** 50mm (2in).
● **Diet:** Insect larvae, aquatic worms and most small crustaceans and invertebrates.
● **Sex differences:** Males are smaller than females.
● **Aquarium breeding:** This species has not spawned in the aquarium.
● **Aquarium compatibility:** Peaceful.

This delightful and attractive Brazilian catfish – its silver-white body adorned with fine black dots – is much confused with the Peruvian species *Corydoras trilineatus* (see page 83).

*Corydoras julii* is a small, delicate species suited only to small, peaceful community aquariums. It is not too demanding of specific water quality and will thrive in acidic to neutral pH levels.

## Corydoras leopardus
*Leopard Catfish*
● **Habitat:** Colombian and Brazilian rivers.
● **Length:** 75mm (3in).
● **Diet:** Insect larvae, aquatic worms and most small crustaceans and invertebrates.
● **Sex differences:** Males are more slender than females.
● **Aquarium breeding:** Has not

spawned in the aquarium.
● **Aquarium compatibility:**
Peaceful.

At 75mm (3in), the Leopard Catfish is larger than the two species with which it is sometimes confused; *Corydoras julii* and *Corydoras trilineatus*. All three species have a black dorsal spot and the same basic body pattern.

Above: **Corydoras julii**
*This beautiful Brazilian species is easily maintained in slightly acidic waters. It is best suited to the small community aquarium.*

Below: **Corydoras leopardus**
*Another peaceful community catfish that is very adaptable to a broad range of water conditions and different sizes of aquarium.*

## Corydoras leucomelas
*False Spotted Catfish*
● **Habitat:** Colombian and Peruvian rivers.
● **Length:** 50mm (2in).
● **Diet:** Insect larvae, aquatic worms and most small crustaceans and invertebrates.
● **Sex differences:** Males are smaller than females.
● **Aquarium breeding:** Has not spawned in the aquarium.
● **Aquarium compatibility:** Peaceful.

This widespread species can be identified by its eye mask and dorsal shoulder blotch. It is closest to *Corydoras ambiacus*, which shares the same basic colour pattern but grows larger.

## Corydoras melanistius melanistius
*Spotted Catfish*
● **Habitat:** Rivers in Guyana.
● **Length:** 65mm (2.5in).
● **Diet:** Insect larvae, aquatic worms and most small crustaceans and invertebrates.
● **Sex differences:** Males are smaller than females.
● **Aquarium breeding:** Egg laying. This species is found in huge numbers in Guyanan rivers but is very rarely spawned in the aquarium. The fishes spawn over a 24 hour period, and eggs are placed on the leaves of plants or on the aquarium glass.
● **Aquarium compatibility:** Peaceful.

*Corydoras melanistius* is the main species exported from Guyana and is similar in appearance to several spotted species. It is probably one of the top five best-known *Corydoras* species. A subspecies, *Corydoras melanistius brevirostris* is distinguished by the patterning, several black stripes, in its caudal fin. *Corydoras melanistius melanistius* has black speckles across the head and body, a black band across the eye and dorsal fin, and a clear caudal fin.

Below: **Corydoras melanistius melanistius**
*The popular Spotted Catfish will thrive in neutral water conditions, especially when kept in groups of four or more specimens.*

## Corydoras melanotaenia
*Green Gold Catfish*
● **Habitat:** Colombian rivers.
● **Length:** 75mm (3in).
● **Diet:** Insect larvae, aquatic worms and most small crustaceans and invertebrates.
● **Sex differences:** Males are distinctly more slender than females.
● **Aquarium breeding:** This species is very closely related to the Bronze Catfish (see page 64), but is not as easily bred. Spawning can be induced by adding cool water to the aquarium. Egg laying, as with all *Corydoras* catfishes.
● **Aquarium compatibility:** Peaceful.

Above: **Corydoras leucomelas**
*A small shy species, ideal for the modest community aquarium.*

Below: **Corydoras melanotaenia**
*These fast swimmers are happiest in large community aquariums with bright, slightly alkaline water.*

The Green Gold Catfish has often been confused with the Bronze Catfish, *Corydoras aeneus*, but its common name highlights the difference in colour pattern. It is also longer in the head and body than *C. aeneus*. This small, shy species would be a welcome addition to the community aquarium.

## Corydoras melini
*False Bandit Catfish*
● **Habitat:** Colombian and Brazilian waters.
● **Length:** 50mm (2in).
● **Diet:** Insect larvae, aquatic worms and most small crustaceans and invertebrates.
● **Sex differences:** Females are more robust than males.
● **Aquarium breeding:** Egg production rarely exceeds 20-30 and these are placed in and among plants, where they can be easily overlooked on the undersides of the leaves.
● **Aquarium compatibility:** An excellent community species.

This species is easily confused with *Corydoras metae*, with which it shares the Rio Meta Basin waters. If you look closely, you will see that the stripe continues into the tail fin in *C. melini*, whereas in *C. metae* the pattern rounds off at the base of the tail.

## Corydoras metae
*Bandit Catfish; Meta River Catfish*
● **Habitat:** Colombian rivers.
● **Length:** 50mm (2in).
● **Diet:** Insect larvae, aquatic worms and most small crustaceans and invertebrates.
● **Sex differences:** Females are slightly larger than males.
● **Aquarium breeding:** About 0-30 eggs are placed on plants d/or on the aquarium glass.
**quarium compatibility:**
eful.

Above: **Corydoras melini**
*This catfish shares the eye stripe and body pattern with several species, including a new Brazilian form named after the author.*

The Bandit Catfish is one of the most popular Colombian species. It has a lookalike, aptly called *Corydoras simulatus*, which has a longer snout.

The two species are imported together and it is worth keeping an eye on new batches in the aquarium shop to spot the mimics.

## Corydoras nattereri
*Natterer's Catfish*
● **Habitat:** Coastal rivers of Brazil.
● **Length:** 50mm (2in).
● **Diet:** Insect larvae, aquatic worms and most small crustaceans and invertebrates.
● **Sex differences:** Females are more rotund than males.
● **Aquarium breeding:** One of the easiest of the wild forms to spawn. Large females can produce up to 200 eggs, which hatch within 24-36 hours at 26°C (79°F). Fry are hardy, with a low fatality rate.
● **Aquarium compatibility:** Peaceful.

This blue catfish is imported from southern Brazil in great quantities and has been spawned by many fishkeepers. *Corydoras nattereri* is a very robust and undemanding species which will live quite comfortably in both acidic and slightly alkaline water.

Above: **Corydoras metae**
*A bright water catfish which shares the same rivers as* C. melini, *and its mimic,* C. simulatus.

Below: **Corydoras nattereri**
*Extremely robust and easily bred; this species will adapt to a broad range of water conditions.*

## Corydoras paleatus
*Peppered Catfish*
● **Habitat:** Brazilian and Argentinian rivers.
● **Length:** 100mm (4in).
● **Diet:** Insect larvae, aquatic worms and most small crustaceans and invertebrates.
● **Sex differences:** Females are much larger than males.
● **Aquarium breeding:** The farm-raised forms spawn easily, but breeding large wild fishes proves more difficult.
● **Aquarium compatibility:** This peaceful Brazilian beauty is frequently included in the home community aquarium.

Farmed in the Far East and Florida, the grey and black blotched Peppered Catfish is one of the most popular species available to fishkeepers. The farm-raised specimens are extremely hardy and adaptable, and are suited to the majority of community aquariums. As with virtually all *Corydoras* species, they are most active when kept in small groups of between three and six specimens. It was originally collected by Charles Darwin on the voyage of the Beagle in the 1830s.

Below: **Corydoras paleatus**
*The several colour forms of this species include this Brazilian one.*

## Corydoras panda
*Panda Catfish*
● **Habitat:** Peruvian rivers.
● **Length:** 50mm (2in).
● **Diet:** Insect larvae, aquatic worms and most small crustaceans and invertebrates.
● **Sex differences:** Females are slightly larger than males.
● **Aquarium breeding:** Spawning takes place over a 12-24 hour period and about 20-30 eggs are placed on the glass. These are best hatched in a separate dish or breeding trap (see Breeding section, page 49).
● **Aquarium compatibility:** Peaceful.

Above: **Corydoras panda**
*Now widely available, these striking catfishes have become firm favourites with enthusiasts.*

This catfish has recently been imported from Peru by enterprising wholesalers. The attractive 'panda' eye mask and tail spot make it one of the most sought after of all catfishes, but, because of its rarity, it is very expensive. Pairs or larger groups can be kept in a community aquarium with bright, clear, neutral water. Once they reach maturity you can isolate a pair to a small breeding aquarium (see Breeding section).

## Corydoras pygmaeus
*Pigmy Catfish*
● **Habitat:** Rivers in Brazil and Peru.
● **Length:** 25mm (1in).
● **Diet:** Fine invertebrates and organic foods.
● **Sex differences:** Males are smaller and more slender than females.
● **Aquarium breeding:** There are many reports of Pigmy Catfishes spawning and fry being raised in community aquariums without any direct intervention by fishkeepers.
● **Aquarium compatibility:** Small species such as this are best kept in small community aquariums or in breeding tanks as larger fishes are likely to mistake them for food!

This species is often confused with another pigmy species, *Corydoras hastatus*. Although alike, the body stripe in *Corydoras pygmaeus* is distinctive from the tail spot pattern of *Corydoras hastatus* (see page 70). The Pigmy Catfish, found in midwater shoals of thousands in the wild, will only thrive if kept in groups in the aquarium. This tiny fish will accept a wide range of conditions and is adaptable to extremes in water hardness.

Below: **Corydoras pygmaeus**
*The best-known pigmy species and easily bred in small aquariums.*

## Corydoras rabauti
*Rabaut's Catfish*
● **Habitat:** Peruvian and Brazilian rivers.
● **Length:** 50mm (2in).
● **Diet:** Insect larvae, aquatic worms and most small crustaceans and invertebrates.
● **Sex differences:** Females are slightly larger than males.
● **Aquarium breeding:** Fairly easy to spawn with a cool water trigger (see page 44).
● **Aquarium compatibility:** Peaceful.

*Corydoras rabauti* (also known as *C. myersi*) produces some of the prettiest fry of all the *Corydoras* species; the juveniles display a red-brown band around the middle of the body, which they lose in maturity. This species is constantly confused with *Corydoras zygatus* from Peru, which has an identical colour pattern but grows larger. The fry are different, however, as *C. zygatus* young have the same pattern as the adults.

Below: **Corydoras rabauti**
*A small and peaceful Brazilian species which is ideally suited to a quiet community aquarium.*

## Corydoras reticulatus
*Network Catfish*
● **Habitat:** Peruvian rivers.
● **Length:** 50mm (2in).
● **Diet:** Insect larvae, aquatic worms and most small crustaceans and invertebrates.
● **Sex differences:** Males are smaller than females.
● **Aquarium breeding:** Very difficult to spawn in the aquarium.
● **Aquarium compatibility:** A peaceful fish which will thrive in shoals of its own kind or other small species.

The Network Catfish was thought to have a great many colour forms until, in 1986, one of the so-called *Corydoras reticulatus* forms was described as a new species, *Corydoras sodalis* (see page 80). However, as is the case with many of the species described, the colour pattern would still seem to be variable. The Network Catfish has a longer head than its mimic, dark reticulations in the body, and a dorsal spot.

Right: **Corydoras reticulatus**
*The Network Catfish prefers bright, neutral water conditions and is happiest kept in a shoal.*

# Corydoras robineae
*Mrs Schwartz's Catfish; Flagtail Corydoras*

● **Habitat:** Whitewater tributaries of the Rio Negro.
● **Length:** 75mm (3in).
● **Diet:** Insect larvae, aquatic worms and most small crustaceans and invertebrates.
● **Sex differences:** Males are more slender than females.
● **Aquarium breeding:** There are no records of successful breedings of this relative newcomer to the aquarium.

Above: **Corydoras robineae**
*A recently discovered favourite.*

● **Aquarium compatibility:** Peaceful.

The Flagtail Corydoras has been imported in fairly large numbers in recent years. Only discovered in 1983, it is now firmly fixed in the enthusiasts' list of great species.

It possesses a distinctive caudal pattern, which it shares with its larger relative, *Dianema urostriata* (see page 84).

## Corydoras schwartzi
*Mr Schwartz's Catfish*
● **Habitat:** Brazilian rivers.
● **Length:** 60mm (2.4in).
● **Diet:** Insect larvae, aquatic worms and most small crustaceans and invertebrates.
● **Sex differences:** Difficult to sex, but females are generally more rotund than males.
● **Aquarium breeding:** Difficult to spawn in the aquarium.
● **Aquarium compatibility:** Peaceful.

*Corydoras schwartzi* prefers slightly acidic pH levels and is best kept in fairly soft water. It is a hardy and robust fish, and so can be kept in a community aquarium with larger fishes. The common name of this species stems from the late great Brazilian fish exporter, whose business is now handled by Mrs Schwartz and her son Adolf Schwartz. The family now have three *Corydoras* catfishes named after them.

Below: **Corydoras schwartzi**
*Although fairly hardy, this species prefers acidic conditions and is unsuited to newly established neutral water aquariums.*

Right: **Corydoras sodalis**
*This attractive pair will live happily alongside* Corydoras reticulatus, *which they mimic.*

## Corydoras sodalis
*False Network Catfish*
● **Habitat:** Small offshoots of large creeks and rivers in Peru and Brazil.
● **Length:** 50mm (2in).
● **Diet:** Insect larvae, aquatic worms and most small crustaceans and invertebrates.
● **Sex differences:** Males are more slender and less robust than females.
● **Aquarium breeding:** Not known, but is likely to be typical of most species of *Corydoras*.
● **Aquarium compatibility:** Peaceful.

*Corydoras sodalis* is invariably confused with *Corydoras reticulatus* (see page 78).
*C. sodalis* has a shorter, more rounded profile, lighter reticulation, and only light pigment in the dorsal fin. Keeping these two species together in the aquarium is, thankfully, not a problem, as both thrive in neutral to slightly alkaline waters and are relatively robust and undemanding.

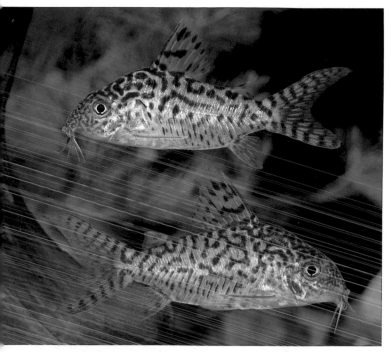

## Corydoras sychri
*Sychr's Catfish*
● **Habitat:** Peruvian rivers.
● **Length:** 50mm (2in).
● **Diet:** Insect larvae, aquatic worms and most small crustaceans and invertebrates.
● **Sex differences:** Males are smaller than females.
● **Aquarium breeding:** There are no reports of fishes spawning in the aquarium.
● **Aquarium compatibility:** Peaceful.

The eye mask and fine body spots help to distinguish this catfish from other species. Imports have been sporadic since 1975, but occasionally specimens arrive with other fishes from Peru or Ecuador. The fishes, like many other species, may be delicate on import and should be given bright, clear, neutral water. Once settled in the aquarium, however, they are less demanding of water conditions.

Below: **Corydoras sychri**
*This species is not regularly available and can be somewhat delicate on import, but individuals generally prove easy to keep once they are settled in the aquarium.*

## Corydoras treitlii
*Hognosed Corydoras*
● **Habitat:** Brazilian rivers.
● **Length:** 75mm (3in).
● **Diet:** Insect larvae, aquatic worms and most small crustaceans and invertebrates.
● **Sex differences:** Difficult to sex, but males are slightly smaller than females.
● **Aquarium breeding:** This catfish was spawned for the first time in an aquarium in 1986. In the wild, these fishes lay a few eggs, which they place among plants.

● **Aquarium compatibility:** Peaceful.

This long-nosed species is usually found as an odd one among other fishes in Brazilian imports. It tends to be more secretive than those species with a shorter head length, and will retreat into the plants at the slightest sound.

Below: **Corydoras treitlii**
*This rare species can be spawned in the aquarium, as shown by the youngster and parents here.*

# Corydoras trilineatus
*Three Line Catfish*
● **Habitat:** Widespread in Peruvian, Brazilian and Colombian rivers.
● **Length:** 50mm (2in).
● **Diet:** Insect larvae, aquatic worms and most small crustaceans and invertebrates.
● **Sex differences:** Difficult to sex, but adult females are generally more robust than males.
● **Aquarium breeding:** Although imports are common, this species remains difficult to spawn in captivity. Many eggs are produced when spawnings are successful.
● **Aquarium compatibility:** Peaceful.

The hardy nature and attractive pattern of the Three Line Catfish make it very popular with fishkeepers. The species has been confused with the Brazilian *Corydoras julii* (see page 70) since fishkeeping began. *Corydoras trilineatus* is a robust species possessing a distinctive mid body lateral stripe bordered so as to create the impression of three lines. (*Corydoras julii* is small and delicate in comparison, and has an even pigment patterning of tiny black spots.) Although plentiful in nature and extremely hardy in the aquarium, *Corydoras trilineatus* has proved very difficult to spawn in captivity. Peruvian species are known to prefer bright, neutral pH water and this might be the key to successful breeding.

# Corydoras zygatus
*Black Band Catfish*
● **Habitat:** Peruvian rivers.
● **Length:** 75mm (3in).
● **Diet:** Insect larvae, aquatic worms and most small crustaceans and invertebrates.
● **Sex differences:** Females are larger than males.
● **Aquarium breeding:** Fine; will produce six hundred eggs in one spawning.
● **Aquarium compatibility:** Peaceful.

This tan-bodied, black-striped species is often confused with *C. rabauti* (see page 78). It was once easily obtainable but imports have become scarce since 1985 because of the unfavourable political climate in Peru – its country of origin.

Left: **Corydoras trilineatus**
*Ideal for the community aquarium, the Three Line Catfish will adapt to a broad range of conditions.*

Below: **Corydoras zygatus**
*This robust species will soon develop into spawning condition in a large community aquarium.*

## Dianema longibarbis
*Porthole Catfish*
● **Habitat:** Peruvian and Brazilian creeks, ponds and rivers.
● **Length:** 100mm (4in).
● **Diet:** Small invertebrates.
● **Sex differences:** Males are more slender than females.
● **Aquarium breeding:** *Dianema* are the only catfishes in this family in which spawning remains a mystery.
● **Aquarium compatibility:** Peaceful.

The Porthole Catfish resembles an elongated *Corydoras* and shares the peaceful character of its cousins. Some fishkeepers have suggested that *Dianema* may spawn in the bubblenest fashion of *Hoplosternum*, but this has not been proven.

Above: **Dianema longibarbis**
*The clear caudal fin distinguishes this species from the Flagtail.*

## Dianema urostriata
*Flagtail Catfish*
● **Habitat:** Brazilian rivers, creeks and pools.
● **Length:** 125-150mm (5-6in).
● **Diet:** Small invertebrates.
● **Sex differences:** Males are more slender than females and may show thickened pectoral spines.
● **Aquarium breeding:** Not known.
● **Aquarium compatibility:** Peaceful; an ideal larger catfish for the community aquarium.

Below: **Dianema urostriata**
*One of the few callichthyids yet to be spawned in the aquarium.*

The popular Flagtail Catfishes are known to shoal in large numbers in the wild and thrive when kept together in a reasonably large aquarium (at least 120cm/48in long). Acidic softwater conditions are best for this species, particularly as newly imported specimens are likely to be susceptible to disease and stress-related infections if introduced into hard alkaline waters.

## Hoplosternum thoracatum

*Bubblenest Catfish*
● **Habitat:** Large rivers and swamps from northern South America (Guyana-Surinam) to Brazil.
● **Length:** 200mm (8in).
● **Diet:** Crustaceans and small invertebrates.

Above:
**Hoplosternum thoracatum**
*This form does not retain its attractive speckled patterning in mature condition.*

● **Sex differences:** Males have thickened pectoral spines and are slightly smaller and darker in colour than females when in breeding condition.
● **Aquarium breeding:** The male constructs a bubblenest in which the fertilized eggs are placed.
● **Aquarium compatibility:** Peaceful.

This speckled catfish is especially attractive in juvenile colours; in adults, the speckled pattern begins to fade. It is one of three species of *Hoplosternum* known to fishkeepers and is particularly popular among catfish breeders.

Family: DORADIDAE Talking Catfishes

The Talking, or Thorny, Catfishes are closely related to the scaleless Driftwood Catfishes, except that, unlike the latter, they possess a single row of bony plates along the body flanks. Smaller forms in this family include the well-known *Platydoras* and *Amblydoras*, which are non-predatory towards other fishes and are thus ideal for the community aquarium. The larger forms are almost prehistoric in shape and in their possession of scute thorns (body spines) although they are harmless opportunist feeders living on fruit, snails and seeds. Smaller forms, such as *Agamyxis*, have been known to spawn in the aquarium, but this is an extremely rare occurrence.

## Agamyxis pectinifrons
*Spotted Talking Catfish*
● **Habitat:** Widespread throughout South American rivers.
● **Length:** 125mm (5in).
● **Diet:** Crustaceans and invertebrates.
● **Sex differences:** Females are deeper bodied than males.
● **Aquarium breeding:** It will spawn among floating plants in the aquarium.
● **Aquarium compatibility:** Safe with fishes of equal size.

is Brazilian catfish is black with ʼow or white spots across the

Above: **Agamyxis pectinifrons**
*No two specimens of this intriguing catfish are identical. Some are lightly patterned with spots, in some the spots form lines, and others are finely peppered.*

body. As with all doradids, this species is inactive during daylight hours although you can encourage the fishes to appear by introducing freshly shredded shrimps and prawns, which they relish. Ensure adequate hiding places for these fishes by constructing caves and crevices from rocks and pieces of bogwood in the aquarium.

## Amblydoras hancocki
*Hancock's Catfish*
● **Habitat:** Widespread in rivers from Guyana to Brazil.
● **Length:** 100mm (4in).
● **Diet:** Crustaceans and invertebrates.
● **Sex differences:** Females are deeper bodied than males.
● **Aquarium breeding:** Scanty reports suggest substrate 'nest' spawnings, although habitat observations by Hancock, published in 1829, state that these catfishes spawn in the rains after making a nest of leaves, and that parental care is shown. From recent reports it seems likely that this species will also spawn in floating plants.
● **Aquarium compatibility:** Safe with fishes of equal size.

The author has seen huge numbers of this species collected in the Essequibo River in Guyana, and awaiting export. Hancock's Catfish is undemanding and seems

Above: **Amblydoras hancocki**
*A tough smaller doradid, this species is found in great shoals in the main Guyanan rivers and is exported in huge quantities.*

to adapt easily to a wide range of water conditions. However, bright, neutral and soft water and a densely planted aquascape will create ideal conditions.

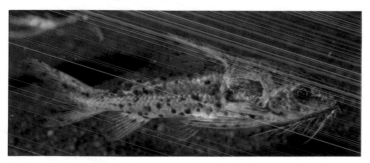

## Opsodoras stubeli
*Feather Barbels Catfish*
● **Habitat:** Rivers in Peru and Ecuador.
● **Length:** 150mm (6in).
● **Diet:** Insect larvae, various aquatic invertebrates and algae.
● **Sex differences:** Females are slightly larger than males.
● **Aquarium breeding:** Not recorded.
● **Aquarium compatibility:** Peaceful.

This unusual catfish, although not colourful, has intriguing feathered barbels and is more active in the

Above: **Opsodoras stubeli**
*Often a fussy feeder in the aquarium, this fish shows a preference for finely shredded shrimp and freeze-dried* Tubifex.

aquarium than other more common species. In an aquarium with subdued lighting, the catfish can be seen sifting through the substrate for small food particles. Once established in a community aquarium, *Opsodoras* is relatively easy to maintain, but regular partial water changes are important for this catfish as it will rarely thrive in poor quality water.

## Platydoras costatus

*Humbug Catfish*
- **Habitat:** Widespread in rivers from Peru to Brazil.
- **Length:** 200mm (8in).
- **Diet:** Snails, insect larvae, etc.
- **Sex differences:** Females are larger than males.
- **Aquarium breeding:** Not recorded.
- **Aquarium compatibility:** The Humbug Catfish can be extremely territorial towards its own kind and is likely to dispute ownership of caves, nooks and crannies with other nocturnal catfishes. However, it is not over aggressive and will do little more than outspread its pectoral and dorsal fin spines and this is only dangerous when directed at scaleless fishes disputing territory.

This black Talking Catfish has a 'humbug' white stripe across its lateral line and this striking pattern makes it popular among fishkeepers seeking an oddity for the community aquarium. Like most catfishes, *Platydoras costatus* is extremely nocturnal.

Above: **Platydoras costatus**
*The best-known doradid, the Humbug Catfish is regularly exported in large quantities.*

## Pseudodoras niger

*Mother of Snails Catfish*
- **Habitat:** Large rivers throughout South America.
- **Length:** 600mm (24in).
- **Diet:** Crustaceans, seeds, fruits and invertebrates.
- **Sex differences:** Not known.
- **Aquarium breeding:** Not known.
- **Aquarium compatibility:** Peaceful.

A 75mm (3in) baby 'niger' will grow into a 600mm (24in) black beauty, given enough space. Despite its large adult size, however, it is a 'gentle giant', one of the few giant catfishes that is perfectly peaceful with small fishes. It is known to eat snails, hence its common name.

Below: **Pseudodoras niger**
*The long snout betrays the identity of this large doradid, sometimes referred to as Oxydoras.*

LORICARIIDAE Suckermouth and Whiptail Catfishes

This family contains more species than any other catfish family, with a great diversity in terms of size, shape and colour. *Hypostomus* and *Pterygoplichthys*, for example, can grow to between 300 and 600mm (12-24in), whereas the tiny *Otocinclus* is adult at only 50mm (2in). These fishes have a wide distribution, encompassing Central as well as South America, and are characterized by their possession of a sucker mouth underneath the head. Some species are also heavily plated. The males of most species are parental towards eggs and fry, and successful aquarium breeding is common. Large forms spawn in riverbank burrows, however, and this site is difficult to recreate successfully in the aquarium.

# Ancistrus dolichopterus
*Bristle-nosed Catfish*
● **Habitat:** Widespread in rivers throughout South America.
● **Length:** 125mm (5in).
● **Diet:** Algae, plants, fruits and small invertebrates.
● **Sex differences:** Males develop distinctive head bristles in the breeding season.
● **Aquarium breeding:** Frequently spawned in community aquariums. Indeed, it is not unusual for the fishkeeper to discover a secret spawning when the youngsters appear from under bogwood at a week or so old. Males are wonderfully parental towards eggs and fry but in the community aquarium it is best to remove fry to a shallow aquarium and feed them with plenty of greenfood (see *Caring for fry*, page 49).
● **Aquarium compatibility:** Territorial among their own kind, but otherwise peaceful.

*Ancistrus dolichopterus* is one of over 50 species of *Ancistrus* known but identification of individual specimens is almost impossible without an array of scientific data. Bristle-nosed Catfishes are superb community aquarium scavengers and, being robust and extremely adaptable, are suited to most water conditions. In the wild they survive in shallow pools which almost dry up outside of the rainy seasons. They feed on algae, which is plentiful in the wild, and this habit is useful in the aquarium, where they can be used to clean the aquarium glass of excess algae. You will need to supplement their diet with greenfoods, such as shredded spinach leaf, green beans, peas and lettuce.

Below: **Ancistrus dolichopterus**
*The male of this species (left) sports cheek bristles in maturity.*

## Chaetostoma thomsonii
*Bulldog Catfish*
- **Habitat:** Fast streams flowing from the Andes through Colombia and Peru.
- **Length:** 100mm (4in).
- **Diet:** Algae and crustaceans.
- **Sex differences:** Males are more patterned than females.
- **Aquarium breeding:** Not recorded.
- **Aquarium compatibility:** Give these fishes plenty of aquarium space; they can be territorial with their own kind.

This species is imported from Colombia in great quantities, but few survive long in the relatively still waters of the aquarium. The Bulldog Catfish has a flat ventral region and the wide sucker mouth, typical of the family – clearly an adaptation to enable the fishes to grip onto rocks in the frothy falls of fast-flowing Andean streams.

Below: **Chaetostoma thomsonii**
*The identity of individuals is always doubtful because of the great number of species known.*

## Farlowella gracilis
*Twig Catfish*
- **Habitat:** Colombian rivers.
- **Length:** 200mm (8in).
- **Diet:** Algae, plants and organic material.
- **Sex differences:** Males are more slender than females.
- **Aquarium breeding:** Accounts of successful spawnings in the aquarium are uncommon. The female places eggs on long-stemmed plants or on the aquarium glass and the male guards them until they hatch.
- **Aquarium compatibility:** ᴇaceful.

only are there almost 60 ⋯ies of *Farlowella* known, most ⋯ch are difficult to differentiate ⋯ch other without close ⋯tion, but there are also several related genera, *Sturisoma* and some species of *Rineloricaria*, which appear remarkably similar. All have long slender bodies and excellent camouflage, as their common name suggests. These fishes prefer an aquarium between 45-60cm (18-24in) deep and will thrive in bright, acidic to neutral water. They will indicate poor water quality, especially low oxygen conditions, by poking their snout above the surface of the water, but will generally prove easy to maintain once they are established in the aquarium.

Right: **Farlowella gracilis**
*Spawnings of these extraordinary and popular fishes are still not common in the aquarium and this catfish continues to represent a challenge to catfish enthusiasts.*

## Hypoptopoma inspectatum

*Giant Otocinclus*

● **Habitat:** Paraguay River.
● **Length:** 75mm (3in).
● **Diet:** Algae, plants and organic material.
● **Sex differences:** Males are more slender than females.
● **Aquarium breeding:** Not recorded.
● **Aquarium compatibility:** Males appear to be territorial but several can be kept together in a large aquarium which is thickly planted.

Above:
**Hypoptopoma inspectatum**
*Note this catfish's distinctive eyes.*

Paraguayan shipments of fishes are enhanced by these 75mm (3in) *Otocinclus*-type Suckermouths. On import they have proved somewhat delicate and high losses have been reported. Feed them daily amounts of softened leaf spinach, which is rich in the nutrients required by loricariids. They show a preference for soft, neutral to alkaline water.

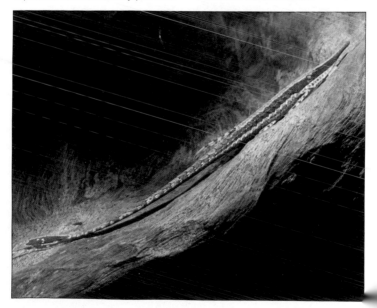

# Hypostomus plecostomus

*Common Plec*

● **Habitat:** Widespread in ponds, creeks, fast and slow rivers throughout South America.
● **Length:** 300mm (12in).
● **Diet:** Plant debris, fruits, algae, crustaceans and invertebrates.
● **Sex differences:** Males are smaller than females.
● **Aquarium breeding:** Breeding is possible only in outdoor ponds because these fishes dig tunnels in which to spawn.
● **Aquarium compatibility:** Territorial among their own kind, but otherwise peaceful.

The 'Plec' is typical of this group of over 120 species of catfishes. Bony platelets replace the normal scales over the whole body, except the ventral region, and act as an effective defensive 'armour'. The characteristic disc-shaped mouth with small flat lips enables the fish to 'suck' onto boulders in fast-flowing water. *Hypostomus* swims in the marginal plants and flooded grasses, sifting through the silt for food and using its teeth to rasp at algae and rich vegetation on the riverbed. This hardy catfish is popular because it will survive a wide range of water conditions and because it is virtually indestructible; it can store air in the gut, which makes it possible for it to survive stagnant conditions that may occur both in the wild and during export.

Above:
**Hypostomus plecostomus**
*Probably the best known and most popular of the larger catfishes.*

# Hypostomus 'ecuador'

*Leopard Plec*

● **Habitat:** Rivers in Ecuador.
● **Length:** 200mm (8in).
● **Diet:** Small aquatic invertebrates, insects and crustaceans, and plant material.
● **Sex differences:** Males have darker markings than females.
● **Aquarium breeding:** Not known.
● **Aquarium compatibility:** Young specimens live together happily and are ideal for any community

Below: **Hypostomus 'ecuador'**
*A newly identified species, shown to the author by Heiko Bleher.*

aquarium. Sexually mature – about 150mm (6in) long – individuals can be very territorial towards both their own kind and other Suckermouth Catfishes.

This Ecuadorian species illustrates the range of colour pattern which can be seen in the genus *Hypostomus*. All seem to be extremely adaptable to a wide variety of water conditions. Individual species are virtually impossible to identify without a full scientific examination of a preserved specimen. Like all species in the genus, *Hypostomus 'ecuador'* is best suited to large community aquariums.

# Loricariichthys platymetapon

*Spoon-head Whiptail*

● **Habitat:** Sandbanks of large Brazilian and Paraguayan creeks and rivers.
● **Length:** 300mm (12in).
● **Diet:** Small aquatic invertebrates, insects and crustaceans, and plant material.
● **Sex differences:** It is possible to distinguish the sexes only during the breeding season, when the male develops enlarged lips to carry the eggs.
● **Aquarium breeding:** There are no spawning accounts. Although some fishkeepers have reported males carrying a few eggs, these have not hatched.
● **Aquarium compatibility:** Ideal for any community.

This unusual large Suckermouth is popular with dedicated catfish enthusiasts and is often included in communities of large South American cichlids and tetras. Large specimens prefer sand as a substrate; they bury themselves, 'alligator-fashion', until only their eyes are visible. This is possibly a protection technique to keep them out of view of predators.

Below:
**Loricariichthys platymetapon**
*A rarity to enhance any aquarium.*

## Otocinclus flexilis
*Peppered Suckermouth*
● **Habitat:** Alongside the Peppered Catfish (*Corydoras paleatus*) in Brazil and Argentina.
● **Length:** 50mm (2in).
● **Diet:** Algae, plants and invertebrates.
● **Sex differences:** Males are more slender than females.
● **Aquarium breeding:** Not recorded.
● **Aquarium compatibility:** There are many reports of hungry *Otocinclus* sucking at the body mucus of other fishes and causing infections. This semi-parasitic behaviour may well cease if plenty of healthy greenfood, such as peas, spinach and lettuce, is provided for these fishes.

*Otocinclus flexilis* are imported alongside, and resemble, *Corydoras paleatus* (see page 76). They are found in huge shoals and are best kept in small groups (although this is not recommended in a heavily planted aquarium as they can destroy soft-leaved plants). They will eat algae on hard-leaved plants (which is beneficial to the plant) and on the aquarium glass, but you should supplement this diet with a continual supply of greenfoods, such as peas, lettuce, spinach and green beans, and soaked flake (which sinks to the substrate quickly). They will thrive in a broad range of water conditions, and should be kept in a small to medium-sized aquarium.

Below: **Otocinclus flexilis**
*This small fish shares its pattern and habitat with* C. paleatus.

## Otocinclus vestitus
*Pigmy Suckermouth*
● **Habitat:** Widespread in Peruvian, Brazilian and Colombian rivers.
● **Length:** 50mm (2in).
● **Diet:** Algae, plants and invertebrates.
● **Sex differences:** Males are more slender than females.
● **Aquarium breeding:** Eggs are placed on plant leaves and on the aquarium glass. Some parental care is shown.
● **Aquarium compatibility:** Like the Peppered Suckermouth, hungry fishes can be parasitic. Feed plenty of greenfood to discourage this behaviour.

This common *Otocinclus* will adapt to most water conditions and is ideal for the small aquarium with an algae problem! You should supplement this diet of algae with

Above: **Otocinclus vestitus**
*This common catfish species tends to be parasitic if underfed.*

greenfoods and soaked flake food. The species has been incorrectly referred to as *Otocinclus affinis*, a catfish that lives alongside *Corydoras nattereri* in the rivers of southern Brazil. It is possible that the Brazilian form of *O.vestitus* is a separate species, *O. vittatus*.

# Panaque nigrolineatus
*Royal Plec*
● **Habitat:** Peru, Colombia, Venezuela and the Amazon Basin.
● **Length:** 600mm (24in).
● **Diet:** Plants, fruits, algae and general aquatic debris.
● **Sex differences:** Males have thickened and bristled pectoral spines in maturity.
● **Aquarium breeding:** Not known.
● **Aquarium compatibility:** Territorial with its own kind but otherwise peaceful.

This Brazilian and Peruvian giant Suckermouth is an impressive fish; it is large, and has distinctive 'pinstripe' patterns and red eyes. There appear to be several pattern variations in juveniles, but it is not clear if all belong to this species. New imports can be extremely hollow-bellied and it is important to offer them a high-fibre diet and similar foods, such as spinach, to help them recover from malnutrition.

Below: **Panaque nigrolineatus**
*Individuals can be difficult to feed as they mature. These giant Suckermouths require large amounts of shrimp and greenfood.*

Right: **Panaque suttoni**
*Note the distinctive eye colour of this attractive Colombian catfish.*

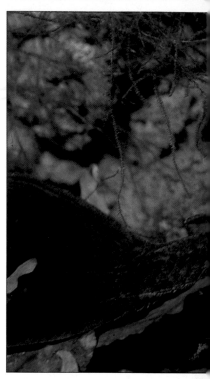

## Panaque suttoni

*Blue-eyed Plec*
● **Habitat:** Colombia.
● **Length:** 450mm (18in).
● **Diet:** Plants, fruits, algae and general aquatic debris.
● **Sex differences:** Males have thickened and bristled pectoral spines in maturity.
● **Aquarium breeding:** Not known.
● **Aquarium compatibility:** Territorial with its own kind but otherwise peaceful.

The Blue-eyed Plec is a quiet, secretive catfish which seems to have special teeth to rasp at vegetation. The biological significance of its bright blue eyes remains a mystery, but they certainly attract fishkeepers! It is often starving on import, and needs extra care. A quarantine aquarium is ideal for this early period, to encourage it to feed.

Right:
**Parotocinclus amazonensis**
*The beautiful False Sucker thrives in a densely planted aquarium.*

## Parotocinclus amazonensis

*False Sucker*
● **Habitat:** Coastal rivers of southern Brazil.
● **Length:** 50mm (2in).
● **Diet:** Algae and invertebrates.
● **Sex differences:** Males are more colourful than females.
● **Aquarium breeding:** Eggs are placed on the leaves of plants.
● **Aquarium compatibility:** Peaceful.

The False Sucker, with its beautiful red-edged fins and long body, is a favourite with enthusiasts. It looks like an *Otocinclus*, but has an adipose fin. New specimens can be difficult to establish but thrive in the community aquarium if provided with bright, neutral soft water and finely shredded spinach.

Right: **Peckoltia pulcher**
*A stunning species known for its territorial behaviour with its own kind; keep this species in groups or singly in a large aquarium.*

## Peckoltia pulcher
*Striped Plec*
- **Habitat:** Highland streams in Colombia and Brazil.
- **Length:** 100mm (4in).
- **Diet:** Algae, invertebrates and large amounts of greenfood on a daily basis.
- **Sex differences:** Males are more colourful than females.
- **Aquarium breeding:** Not known.
- **Aquarium compatibility:** Ideal for the small community aquarium

because of their small adult size, but can be extremely territorial with their own kind. It is unwise to keep several specimens together in an aquarium less than 120cm (48in) in length.

The Striped Plec is much sought after by catfish enthusiasts but is quite rarely imported. It requires bright, neutral water and will flourish with a regular supply of greenfood, such as green beans, spinach and soaked flaked food.

## Peckoltia vittata
*Clown Plec*
- **Habitat:** Brazil.
- **Length:** 75mm (3in).
- **Diet:** Algae, assorted plant material and invertebrates.
- **Sex differences:** Males are slightly smaller and more colourful than females.
- **Aquarium breeding:** Not known.
- **Aquarium compatibility:** Generally peaceful although they can be slightly territorial.

These dwarf Suckermouths are very attractive, usually well marked with stripes and spots, and are sought after by enthusiasts. Although it lacks the rarity value of the Striped Plec, the attractive

Above: **Peckoltia vittata**
*A popular species best suited to small community aquariums.*

Clown Plec is a firm favourite in catfish circles. Its small size and adaptability to almost any range of water conditions, add to its popularity with the fishkeeper.

## Pseudohemiodon laticeps
*Spade Catfish*
- **Habitat:** Paraguayan rivers.
- **Length:** 300mm (12in).

Below: **Pseudohemiodon laticeps**
*A loricariid suitable for the large community, this catfish will thrive if given enough substrate space.*

● **Diet:** Algae, greenfoods and small aquatic invertebrates.
● **Sex differences:** Males are smaller than females.
● **Aquarium breeding:** Not known.
● **Aquarium compatibility:** Peaceful.

This giant Whiptail catfish arrives occasionally in imports. Some specimens have caudal filament extensions longer than the fish itself, but these are usually broken off by fish catchers handling them carelessly. It is important that you regularly supply plenty of food for these larger loricariids – they need far more roughage than their smaller relatives, such as *Otocinclus*.

## Pterygoplichthys anisitsi
*Snow King Plec*
● **Habitat:** Paraguay River.
● **Length:** 600mm (24in).
● **Diet:** Small specimens eat algae and aquatic debris. Large specimens will consume plants, fruits, seeds, snails, dead fish and general organic material, including mud, from which they extract invertebrates.
● **Sex differences:** Males are more brightly patterned and slender than females.
● **Aquarium breeding:** Too large for aquariums, but farms in Florida spawn them in dirt ponds where the catfishes dig burrows and guard the eggs and fry.
● **Aquarium compatibility:** Safe with fishes of equal size.

The Snow King is one of the toughest catfishes from South America and will survive the most extreme water conditions. It has proved adaptable enough to establish itself in the dirt ponds of Florida, where it is part of a large industry farming many thousands every month for a market that thinks of them as Common Plecs. Specimens have even been known to survive in burrows that have been completely exposed above water level in the dry season; providing the burrow is damp, they can survive for weeks and even months. Wild-caught individuals are stunning, with black lines against a white background.

Below: **Pterygoplichthys anisitsi**
*The drab colours of the juvenile Snow King give way to magnificent wavy white lines in maturity.*

## Pterygoplichthys gibbiceps
*Sailfin Plec*
● **Habitat:** Widespread in the Peruvian and Brazilian Amazon.
● **Length:** 450mm (18in).
● **Diet:** They feed avidly on lettuce, peas, spinach, whole prawns and pellets.
● **Sex differences:** Males are more colourful and slender than females.
● **Aquarium breeding:** Not possible in the aquarium. Commercially, this species is spawned in Asian dirt ponds in the same manner as the Snow King.
● **Aquarium compatibility:** Mature specimens are very territorial and can inflict fin damage to others of the same species if confined in too small an aquarium.

Now being farmed in the Far East, this brick-red beauty is one of the top ten most popular catfishes. Adult Sailfins are suited only to large aquariums although juveniles can be kept in more modest-sized tanks providing they are transferred to a larger aquarium as they outgrow their surroundings. Sailfins are highly recommended for the fishkeeper seeking a suitable companion for large South American Cichlids (*Aequidens*, *Geophagus* and *Cichlasoma*) and larger Characins (*Metynnis* Silver Dollars and *Anostomus*-type Pencilfishes).

Right: **Rineloricaria lanceolata**
*One of the most sought after species because of its distinctive shape and colour pattern.*

## Rineloricaria lanceolata
*Whiptail Catfish*
● **Habitat:** Brazil.
● **Length:** 150mm (6in).
● **Diet:** Algae, greenfoods, small aquatic invertebrates and pellets.
● **Sex differences:** Males are more distinctively patterned and more slender than females when viewed from above. Sexually mature males display bristles on the cheek or side of the head.
● **Aquarium breeding:** Eggs are placed in a 50-75mm (2-3in) diameter PVC tube placed in the aquarium (a substitute for the hollow logs in which they spawn in the wild) and are guarded by the male until they hatch.
● **Aquarium compatibility:** Peaceful.

Almost 50 species of these attractively patterned catfishes are known and this Brazilian black dorsal-blotched variety is one of the most sought after. These Whiptail Catfishes enjoy peas, chopped lettuce and spinach.

Below:
**Pterygoplichthys gibbiceps**
*A superb companion for large community cichlids and characins.*

## Rineloricaria lima
*Common Whiptail Catfish*
● **Habitat:** Brazilian rivers.
● **Length:** 180mm (7in).
● **Diet:** Algae, greenfoods and small aquatic invertebrates and pellets.
● **Sex differences:** Males are more distinctively patterned and more slender than females when viewed from above. Sexually mature males display bristles on the cheek or side of the head.
● **Aquarium breeding:** This species is regularly spawned in the aquarium in the same way as *Rineloricaria lanceolata* (see breeding details, left).
● **Aquarium compatibility:** Peaceful.

*Rineloricaria lima*, *R. stewarti* from Guyana to Brazil, and *R. fallax* and *R. lanceolata* from Brazil, are probably the best known of the ten or so species of *Rineloricaria* imported. All make perfect aquarium catfishes. *Rineloricaria* are ideal substrate haunters for the community aquarium. They rarely, if ever, leave the gravel and should therefore be offered tablet food, or presoaked flake (accepted by most catfishes), which will sink directly to the aquarium bottom. This will ensure that they do not miss out on general feedings.

Below: **Rineloricaria lima**
*This species can be kept safely with even very small fishes.*

## Sturisoma aureum
*Giant Whitptail*
- **Habitat:** Colombian rivers.
- **Length:** 300mm (12in).
- **Diet:** Algae, greenfoods and small aquatic invertebrates.
- **Sex differences:** Difficult to sex until maturity when, in the breeding season, males develop cheek bristles. These may be shed after the breeding season, making sexing difficult again.
- **Aquarium breeding:** Eggs are placed on vertical surfaces, such as the aquarium glass or long-leaved plants. The males remain with the eggs until they hatch.
- **Aquarium compatibility:** Slightly territorial with their own kind but can be kept together in a large aquarium. Peaceful with other species and ideal for the community aquarium.

This catfish is also known as *Sturisoma panamese* and, with *S. barbatum*, is one of the most popular large non-predatory catfishes. It has fin extensions almost as long as its body. The species is very easy to breed and the 5mm (2in) babies, all fins and

Above: **Sturisoma aureum**
*This intriguing species, imported in large quantities from Colombia, will grace any community aquarium.*

spindle body, retain their attractive brown and beige striped patterns when they are fully grown.

Above: **Sturisoma barbatum**
*Like its more common relative, S. aureum, this catfish is suitable only for larger aquariums.*

## Sturisoma barbatum
*Giant Twig Catfish*
● **Habitat:** Paraguay River.
● **Length:** 300mm (12in).
● **Diet:** Algae, greenfoods and small aquatic invertebrates.
● **Sex differences:** Males are more slender than females and develop head bristles when sexually mature.
● **Aquarium breeding:** Not known, but assumed to be the same as for *Sturisoma aureum*.
● **Aquarium compatibility:** Peaceful.

This species resembles *S. aureum* but is more slender, almost *Farlowella*-like in shape. Larger aquariums, aquascaped with beechwood branches, are ideal for this Giant Twig Catfish.

*Sturisoma barbatum* make good companions for other robust loricariids in the aquarium, although their fin extensions may be nipped off in territorial disputes or by upper water fishes. They require large amounts of greenfood and spacious bright water conditions to thrive.

PIMELODIDAE Naked Catfishes

These scaleless predators are widely distributed throughout South America. The larger forms inhabit wide, fast-flowing rivers and are characterized by a wide gaping mouth and a broad tail, which aids speed through the water. Smaller forms have tiny eyes, and shoal in huge numbers over the beds of large and small rivers. The family has continued to challenge catfish breeders, as no attempts at spawning or fry raising have yet proved successful.

## Brachyrhamdia imitator
*False Corydoras*
● **Habitat:** Venezuelan rivers.
● **Length:** 75-100mm (3-4in).
● **Diet:** Insect larvae and various invertebrates.
● **Sex differences:** Females are deeper bodied than males.
● **Aquarium breeding:** Unpublished information based on habitat observations and aquarium behaviour suggests that most pimelodids are egg scatterers, but documented details are very scarce.
● **Aquarium compatibility:** Peaceful with fishes of their own size although slightly territorial with each other. They should be fine in a large aquarium.

This is one of three species known to science (the other two, *B. marthae* and *B. meesi*, were discovered and described by the author). They are imported with *Corydoras delphax* and *Corydoras melanistius*, whose patterns they share. Why they 'imitate' *Corydoras* patterns, i.e. in terms of any possible biological or environmental benefit (or similar), is a mystery, although much has been written on the subject. They are active, fast-swimming fishes, and well suited to large aquariums.

Below: **Brachyrhamdia imitator**
*This catfish mimics* Corydoras *so perfectly that certain species are hard to separate at first glance.*

Right: **Brachyrhamdia marthae**
*First described by the author, this species mimics, and is imported with,* Corydoras pygmaeus.

## Brachyrhamdia marthae
*Martha's Catfish*
● **Habitat:** Peruvian and Brazilian Amazon.
● **Length:** 75-100mm (3-4in).
● **Diet:** Insect larvae and various invertebrates.
● **Sex differences:** Females are deeper bodied than males.
● **Aquarium breeding:** Large, swollen specimens have been dissected by the author to reveal thousands of tiny eggs but, as yet, there have been no successful aquarium spawnings.
● **Aquarium compatibility:** Keep this species in a large aquarium; although they are generally peaceful, they may be territorial with their own kind.

This species, although well known to catfish enthusiasts, was only described to science in 1985. It is imported alongside *Corydoras pygmaeus*, with which it shares the same lateral pattern.

## Leiarius marmoratus
*False Perrunichthys*
● **Habitat:** Peruvian and Brazilian Amazon.
● **Length:** 450-500mm (18-20in).
● **Diet:** Small fishes, crustaceans, invertebrates and fruits.
● **Sex differences:** Males are more slender than females.
● **Aquarium breeding:** Not known.
● **Aquarium compatibility:** Give this species plenty of space, because of its large adult size and territorial nature.

For many years, this species was confused with *Perrunichthys*, which is similar but has fewer dorsal rays. This type of predatory catfish requires a large aquarium with a good water flow from power filters, and plenty of swimming space. Once they are mature, such large predatory fishes should not be fed more than twice a week.

## Leiarius pictus
*Sailfin Pim*
● **Habitat:** Brazilian Amazon.
● **Length:** 600mm (24in).
● **Diet:** Small fishes, crustaceans, invertebrates and fruits.
● **Sex differences:** Males are more slender than females.
● **Aquarium breeding:** Not known.
● **Aquarium compatibility:** Two specimens will fight each other and inflict a great deal of fin and body damage in a confined aquarium space.

At 600mm (24in), this long-barbled Brazilian beauty would grace any show aquarium. Imports are now quite rare, although the fish is said to be relatively common in the wild. It should not be mixed with other large pimelodids because of its strongly territorial nature. Large earthworms and small pieces of prawns and freshwater fish will keep this catfish healthy.

Above: **Leiarius pictus**
*The Sailfin is a much sought after catfish for the large display aquarium because of its exceptional finnage and pattern.*

Below: **Leiarius marmoratus**
*Another large predatory catfish suitable for the 'bumper' aquarium, this species has often been confused with* Perrunichthys.

105

## Microglanis iheringi
*Bumble Bee Catfish*
● **Habitat:** Widepread in Peruvian, Venezuelan and Colombian rivers.
● **Length:** 100mm (4in).
● **Diet:** Small aquatic invertebrates.
● **Sex differences:** Males are smaller than females.
● **Aquarium breeding:** Not known.
● **Aquarium compatibility:** Peaceful with fishes larger than itself.

This tiny catfish, with its brown and yellow/beige banding patterns, is not to be confused with the Asian Bumble Bee Catfish, which is much larger. It is very secretive but will make brief skirmishes to the front of the aquarium to feed.

## Perrunichthys perruno
*Perruno Catfish*
● **Habitat:** Venezuelan rivers.
● **Length:** 600mm (24in).
● **Diet:** Small fishes, crustaceans, invertebrates and fruit.

Below: **Microglanis iheringi**
*A dwarf pimelodid, perfect for the smaller community aquarium with plenty of hiding places.*

● **Sex differences:** Not known.
● **Aquarium breeding:** Not known.
● **Aquarium compatibility:** In common with *Leiarius*, this species needs plenty of space; two specimens kept together are likely to fight.

Although generally similar to *Leiarius*, the square head and

dorsal fin of *Perrunichthys* are distinctive features. It is also much rarer than *Leiarius*. Care required and behaviour are similar for both species. Like other larger pimelodids, they are not over fussy with regards to pH and hardness, but they demand bright clean water, so adequate filtration and regular large partial water changes are essential in the aquarium.

Above: **Perrunichthys perruno**
*This huge catfish requires the same care as its cousins, Leiarius.*

## Phractocephalus hemioliopterus
*Red Tail Catfish*
● **Habitat:** Widespread across the Peruvian, Guyanan and Brazilian Amazon.
● **Length:** 1000mm (39in).
● **Diet:** Fish, crustaceans and larger aquatic invertebrates.
● **Sex differences:** Not known, although it is thought that males possess a brighter red tail and are more slender than females.
● **Aquarium breeding:** Not known.
● **Aquarium compatibility:** Must be kept alone, as they will attempt to consume any living creature (and some inanimate objects, such as heaters and suction clips) that they can fit into the mouth.

The Red Tail Catfish is almost a legend among catfish enthusiasts; public aquarium specimens have lived for more than 20 years. Examination of the stomachs of specimens collected in the huge rapids of the Madiera River in Brazil revealed freshwater crabs, fruits and seeds.

Left:
**Phractocephalus hemioliopterus**
*The Emperor of the Amazon and a spectacular public aquarium fish.*

Right: **Pimelodella cristata**
*The Graceful Catfish is a nocturnal predator; feed well on manufactured foods and keep away from small community fishes.*

## Pimelodella cristata

*Graceful Catfish*
● **Habitat:** Widespread.
● **Length:** 200mm (8in).
● **Diet:** Small aquatic invertebrates.
● **Sex differences:** Males sometimes display dorsal filaments and are more slender than females.
● **Aquarium breeding:** Not known.
● **Aquarium compatibility:** Predatory with smaller fishes.

This common species, also known as *P. gracilis* and *P. geryi*, is frequently confused with its larger cousin, *Pimelodus*, but is recognizable by its elongated adipose (second dorsal) fin. Mature specimens of *Pimelodella* may predate on small fishes, but well fed individuals will become rather lazy and rely on manufactured foods. Few fishkeepers are aware of the size they can attain, as aquarium specimens rarely grow beyond 100mm (4in).

## Pimelodus blochi

*Common Pim*
● **Habitat:** Widespread in rivers throughout South America.
● **Length:** 200mm (8in).
● **Diet:** Small fishes, insect larvae and assorted aquatic crustaceans and invertebrates.
● **Sex differences:** Females are deeper bodied than males.
● **Aquarium breeding:** Not known.

Below: **Pimelodus blochi**
*A robust companion for larger South and Central American cichlids in a spacious tank.*

● **Aquarium compatibility:**
Predatory with smaller fishes.

This Common, or Grey Pim, is
found from Brazil to Peru and
shoals in huge numbers in fast-
flowing waters. They can be
territorial, but are usually fine kept
together in groups of three or
more. They are predatory towards
any smaller fishes and are known
to be particularly savage towards
slow, ailing fishes. If well fed on
large prawns, chopped
earthworms, pellet food and large
flakes they make active midwater
shoaling catfishes for large tanks.

Below: **Pimelodus maculatus**
*An attractive, though rarely seen,*
*species which can be kept safely*
*with fishes larger than itself.*

## Pimelodus maculatus
*Spotted Pim*
● **Habitat:** Rivers from Brazil to
Paraguay.
● **Length:** 150mm (6in).
●**Diet:** Small fishes, insect larvae
and assorted aquatic crustaceans.
● **Sex differences:** Not known.
● **Aquarium breeding:** Not
known.
● **Aquarium compatibility:**
Predatory towards smaller fishes

This is one of the more attractively
patterned *Pimelodus* catfishes,
with a silver body similar to that of
the Polka-dot, but with grey/brown
rather than black spots. It seems
to have a wide distribution from
southern Brazil extending into the
Paraguay River in Paraguay. In
Brazil, it is known as *P. clarias*.

Above: **Pimelodus ornatus**
*This beautiful species is, unfortunately, rarely encountered by enthusiasts as Paraguayan shipments are rather uncommon.*

## Pimelodus ornatus
*Ornate Pim*
● **Habitat:** Rivers from Paraguay to Guyana.
● **Length:** 200mm (8in).
● **Diet:** Small fishes, insect larvae and assorted aquatic crustaceans.
● **Sex differences:** Not known.
● **Aquarium breeding:** Not known.
● **Aquarium compatibility:** Large specimens are known to be aggressive and will predate on smaller fishes. However, if well fed on prepared and fresh foods they can become quite docile.

This is a distinctive form in that it is the only *Pimelodus* species to display a dorsal spot. Although it appears to have a wide distribution, the occasional imports are all from the Paraguay River, which flows from southern Brazil, southwards through Paraguay and into Argentina.

## Pimelodus pictus
*Angelica Pim; Polka-dot Catfish;*
● **Habitat:** Peruvian and Colombian rivers.
● **Length:** 125-150mm (5-6in).

● **Diet:** Small fishes, insect larvae, and assorted aquatic crustaceans and invertebrates.
● **Sex differences:** Males are smaller than females.
● **Aquarium breeding:** Not known.
● **Aquarium compatibility:** When introduced to the community aquarium, small fishes, such as neon tetras, may disappear at night, consumed by a hungry *Pimelodus*. Although it will be less predatory if well fed, it is best to keep the *Pimelodus* in an aquarium with larger fishes (see pages 17-19).

This silver-bodied, black-spotted catfish, from the Meta River in Peru and Colombia, is the most popular non-*Corydoras* catfish available to fishkeepers. There are two forms known; the Colombian species has a few indistinct body spots, while the one from Peru is covered in many clearly defined spots. Because of the great number of *Pimelodus* species known, the tentative identification of these species by fish collectors has not been scientifically verified.

Right: **Pimelodus pictus**
*The most popular South American catfish with the exception of the all time favourite* Corydoras.
*However, it is very predatory and so best kept with larger fishes.*

Above:
**Pseudopimelodus raninus**
*This nocturnal predator should not be kept with small community fishes, but is fine with larger fishes.*

## Pseudopimelodus raninus

*Big Bumble Bee Catfish*
● **Habitat:** Peruvian and Brazilian Amazon.
● **Length:** 150mm (6in).
● **Diet:** Small aquatic invertebrates.
● **Sex differences:** Males are more slender than females.

● **Aquarium breeding:** Not known.
● **Aquarium compatibility:** Predatory with smaller fishes.

This is basically a giant *Microglanis. Pseudopimelodus* is undemanding of water conditions but should not be kept in an overcrowded aquarium or bacterial skin infections may result. This catfish is a night-time predator and will consume any unfortunate fish that will fit into its mouth. There are several *raninus* forms, which have been broken into subspecies.

Above:
**Pseudopimelodus zungaro**
*An outstandingly patterned
species imported from Colombia.*

# Pseudopimelodus zungaro

*Giant Bumble Bee Catfish*
● **Habitat:** Widespread in northern
and eastern Colombian rivers.
● **Length:** 200mm (8in).
● **Diet:** Small fishes and aquatic
invertebrates.
● **Sex differences:** Not known.
● **Aquarium breeding:** Not
known.
● **Aquarium compatibility:**
Predatory with small fishes.

These attractively banded
catfishes have distinctive tiny eyes
and are very nocturnal; they are
rarely seen in daylight. *Zungaro*,
like *raninus*, are broken into
subspecies and, again like *raninus*,
are very resilient and thrive in a
broad range of water conditions.
Territorial fishes may dispute the
same cave or hollow in the gravel
and cause damage to their
scaleless bodies, but any
scratches heal very quickly in well-
maintained, properly filtered and
water-changed aquariums.

# Pseudoplatystoma fasciatum

*Tiger Catfish*
● **Habitat:** Widespread in rivers
and lakes across South America.
● **Length:** This catfish is said to
grow up to 2000mm (80in) in the
wild, but captive species are
usually nearer 600mm (24in).

● **Diet:** Fish, crustaceans and
anything unfortunate enough to get
in the way!
● **Sex differences:** Not known.
● **Aquarium breeding:** Not known.
● **Aquarium compatibility:**
Predatory; unsafe with anything
other than large characins such as
the Piranha-like *Pacu* etc.

Young specimens can be
encouraged to feed on earthworms
and small pieces of shrimp and
freshwater fish (such as trout) but
adult fishes seem to require
livefood. The huge size of the Tiger
Catfish may scare people off
fishkeeping! Keeping a Tiger
Catfish is, in fact, an art known to
few catfish enthusiasts. It should
only be fed when it displays
hunger by hovering around at the
water surface or reacting to your

Below:
**Pseudoplatystoma fasciatum**
*The huge predatory 'Tiger' reigns
supreme in the giant aquarium.*

presence around the aquarium. Once fed, it will digest its food over a period of days and rest like a large Boa snake. Large specimens can be tamed and will respond to a regular pattern of feeding. Part of the aquarium should have subdued lighting and a large branch under which the catfish can rest. Some fishkeepers, the author included, question the keeping of such large, fastwater catfishes (*Phractocephalus* is another good example) in an aquarium, as only the largest public aquarium can accommodate them adequately. Nevertheless, they are imported for aquariums, and specimens have been kept for many years.

## Sorubim lima

*Shovel-nosed Catfish*
● **Habitat:** Widespread.
● **Length:** 450mm (18in).
● **Diet:** Small fishes.
● **Sex differences:** Not known.
● **Aquarium breeding:** Not known.

Above: **Sorubim lima**
*The most adaptable of the larger pimelodids, this big fish will thrive in most water conditions.*

● **Aquarium compatibility:** Keep with only larger fishes.

The common Shovel-nosed Catfish is one of the few predatory species that can be easily weaned off live fishes. It soon loses the predatory instinct when foods such as shrimp, fish pieces and earthworms are offered on a regular basis. *Sorubim lima* will thrive in a broad range of pH and hardness conditions, demanding only bright well-filtered water. They appear to be one of the few larger pimelodids that can be kept together in small groups, especially if introduced as juveniles. Plenty of aeration and regular generous partial water changes will help to ensure the growth and development of this species in captivity.

# Index to species

Page numbers in **bold** indicate major references, including accompanying photographs. Page numbers in *italics* indicate captions to other illustrations. Less important text entries are shown in normal type.

## A

Adolph's Catfish **64**
*Aequidens* 15, 100
   *A. curviceps 18*
*Agamyxis* 48, 86
   *A. pectinifrons* **86**
*Agmus 14*, 15, 22, 33
   *A. lyriformis* **52**
*Amblydoras 14*, 15, 22, 86
   *A. hancocki 18*, **87**
*Ancistrus 14, 14*, 22, 35, 44, 47
   *A. dolichopterus* **89**
Angelica Pim *18*, **110**
*Anostomus* 15, *18*, 100
   *A. anostomus 18*
Ariidae *17*, 17, **52**
*Arius* 17, 53
   *A. seemani 17*, **53**
Armoured Catfishes 59, **62**
Asian Barbs 49
Asian Bumble Bee Catfish 106
*Aspidoras* 12, *14*, 47, 60
   *A. albater* **59**
   *A. pauciradiatus* 59, **60**
Aspredinidae *14*, 15, *16*, 16, **52-4**
*Aspredo 16*, *48*, 49, 53
   *A. cotylephorus* 16, **53**
*Auchenipterichthys 16*
   *A. thoracatus* 17, **54**, *55*
Auchenipteridae *14*, 15, *16*, 17, **54-8**
Auchenipterids 32, 36, 49, 56

## B

Badger Fishes 15
Bandit Catfish **74**
Banjo Catfishes *14*, 15, *16*, 22, **52-4**
Barbs 18, 21
Bearded Catfish **66**
*Betta splendens* 62
Bicoloured Banjo 15, **54**
Big Bumble Bee Catfish **111**
Black Band Catfish **83**
Black Pigmy Driftwood *57*
Black Top Catfish **62**
Blue-eyed Plec **96**
Bond's Catfish **67**
Bowline Catfish 66
*Brachyplatystoma* 11, 22
*Brachyrhamdia 14*, 15, 49
   *B. imitator 18*, **103**
   *B. marthae* 103, **104**
   *B. meesi* 103
Bristle-nosed Catfish 14, 22, 35, 44, 47, **89**
Britski's Catfish **60**
*Brochis* 12, *14*, 47, 60
   *B. britskii Endpapers*, **60**
   *B. coeruleus* 61
   *B. multiradiatus* 60, **62**
   *B. splendens 18*, **61**

Bronze Catfish **64**, 73
Bubblenest Catfish **85**
Bulldog Catfish 22, **90**
Bumble Bee Catfish **106**
*Bunocephalus 14*, 15, 22, 49
   *B. amaurus 18*, **54**

## C

Callichthyidae 12, *14*, 15, *16*, 46, **59-85**
*Callichthys* 15, *16*, 33, 47, 59, 62
   *C. callichthys* **62**
*Carnegiella marthae 18*
Carp 21
*Chaetostoma* 22, 32
   *C. thomsonii* **90**
Characins 10, 21, 100, 112
*Chilodus punctatus 18*
*Cichlasoma* 15, 100
Cichlids 18
Clown Plec 14, **98**
Colombian Shark Catfish 17
Common Driftwood *56*
Common Pim **108**, 109
Common Plec 15, 16, 22, **92**, 99
Common Whiptail Catfish **101**
*Corydoras* 11, 12, *13*, *14*, 15, 22, *23*, *46*, 46, 47, 59, 60, 61, 62-83, 84, 103
   *C. acutus 18*, **62**
   *C. adolfoi* **64**
   *C. aeneus* 12, *18*, 44, 46, **64**, *65*, 73
      *C. a. schultzi* 64
   *C. ambiacus* **65**, 72
   *C. arcuatus* **66**
   *C. australe* 70
   *C. barbatus 18*, 46, **66**
   *C. blochi* 68
   *C. bondi* **67**
      *C. b. bondi* 67
      *C. b. coppenamensis* 67
   *C. cochui* 69
   *C. delphax Title page,* **68**, 103
   *C. elegans* 46, 68
   *C. habrosus* **69**
   *C. hastatus 13*, 33, **70**, 77
   *C. imitator* 64
   *C. julii* 62, **70**, *71*, 71, 83
   *C. leopardus* **70-1**
   *C. leucomelas* **72**, *73*
   *C. macropterus* **59**, 59
   *C. melanistius* 72, 103
      *C. m. brevirostris* 72
      *C. m. melanistius* **72**
   *C. melanotaenia* **73**
   *C. melini* **74**
   *C. metae* **74**, *75*
   *C. myersi* **78**
   *C. nattereri* **74**, 95
   *C. paleatus* 12, *18*, *44*, 44, *46*, 46, **76**, 94
   *C. panda* **76-7**, *77*
   *C. pygmaeus* 33, 46, 70, **77**, 104
   *C. rabauti* **78**, 83
   *C. reticulatus* **78**, 80
   *C. robinae* **79**
   *C. schwartzi* **80**
   *C. simulatus* **74**, 74
   *C. sodalis* 78, **80**

*C. sychri* **81**
*C. treitlii* **82**
*C. trilineatus* *18*, 70, 71, **83**
*C. zygatus* 78, **83**
Craggy Headed Catfishes 15
Craggy Headed Banjo **52**

# D

*Dianema* 15, *16*, 59
 *D. longibarbis* *18*, **84**
 *D. urostriata* *18*, 79, **84-5**
Doradidae *14*, 15, *16*, 17, **86-8**
Doradids 15, 22, 32, 35, 36, 56
Driftwood Catfishes *14*, 15, *16*, 17, 32, 35, 49, **54-8**, 86
Dwarf Armoured Catfishes *14*, *16*, 46, 59
Dwarf Driftwood Catfishes 15, 33
Dwarf Pimelodid *106*
Dwarf Suckermouth 98

# E

Eel Banjo Catfishes 16, 49, **53**
Eel Driftwood 58, *59*
Elegant Catfish **68**
Emerald Catfish 12, **61**
Emperor of the Amazon 18, *107*
*Entomocurus benjamini* **54**, *55*

# F

False Bandit Catfish **74**
False Blochi Catfish **68**
False Corydoras **60**, **103**
False Macropterus **59**
False Network Catfish **80**
False Perrunichthys **104**
False Spotted Catfish **72**
False Sucker **96**
*Farlowella* 13, *14*, 22, 47, 103
 *F. gracilis* *18*, **90**
Feather Barbels Catfish **87**
Flagtail Catfish **84**
Flagtail Corydoras 79

# G

*Geophagus* 15, 100
Giant Bumble Bee Catfish **112**
Giant Doradids 22
Giant Otocinclus **91**
Giant Talking Catfish 17
Giant Twig Catfish **103**
Giant Whiptail 16, 99, **102**, 103
Gouramies 18
Graceful Catfish **108**
Green Gold Catfish **73**
Grey Pim 109
Guyanan Pigmy Driftwood 58

# H

Hancock's Catfish **87**
Hatchetfishes 10
*Hemigrammus ocellifer* *18*
Hognosed Brochis **62**
Hognosed Corydoras **82**
*Hoplosternum* 15, *16*, 33, 47, 59, *62*, 62, 84
 *H. thoracatum* 47, **85**

Humbug Catfish **88**
*Hyphessobrycon pulchripinnis* 18
*Hypoptopoma* *14*, 15, 22, 48
 *H. inspectatum* **91**
*Hypostomus* 15, 22, *35*, *48*, 48, 89
 *H. 'ecuador'* **92-3**
 *H. plecostomus* *13*, 15, *16*, *18*, **92**

# J

Jaguar Catfish 17, **56**
Julii Catfish **72**

# K

Knifefishes 21

# L

*Leiarius* 17, 18, 106, 107
 *L. marmoratus* **104**, *105*
 *L. pictus* *13*, 18, **104-5**
Leopard Catfish 70, *71*
Leopard Plec **92**
*Leporinus* 15
 *L. affinis* *18*
*Liosomadoras oncinus* *16*, 17, *18*, **56**
Loaches 21
*Loricariichthys* 48
 *L. platymetapon* **93**
Loricariidae 12, *14*, 15, *16*, 47, **89-103**
Loricariids 15, 16, 22, 47, 48

# M

Martha's Catfish **104**
Meta River Catfish **74**
*Metynnis* 15, 100
*Microglanis* *14*, 15, *18*, 49, 111
 *M. iheringi* *18*, **106**
Midnight Catfish 54, *55*
Mother of Snails Catfish **88**
Mr. Schwartz's Catfish **80**
Mrs. Schwartz's Catfish **79**
*Myleus colossoma* 15
 *M. rubripinnis rubripinnis* *18*

# N

Naked Catfishes 11, *14*, 15, *17*, **103-113**
*Nannostomus trifasciatus* *18*
Natterer's Catfish **74**
Network Catfish **78**

# O

*Opsodoras stubeli* **87**
Ornate Pim **110**
*Otocinclus* *14*, 15, 22, 48, 89, 91, 94, 96, 104
 *O. affinis* **95**
 *O. flexilis* **94**
 *O. vestitus* *18*, **94-5**
 *O. vittatus* **95**
*Oxydoras* **88**

# P

*Panaque* 15
 *P. nigrolineatus* *16*, 16, **95**
 *P. suttoni* *16*, 16, **96**
Panda Catfish **76**
*Paracheirodon innesi* *18*
*Parauchenipterus* *16*, 17, 54

*P. galeatus* **56-7**
*Parotocinclus* 48
   *P. amazonensis* **96**
*Paulicea* 11, *13*
*Peckoltia 14*, 14, 47
   *P. pulcher 18*, *96*, **97**
   *P. vittata* **98**
Pencilfishes 10, 100
Peppered Catfish **76**, 94
Peppered Suckermouth **94**
*Perrunichthys 17*, 18, 104, 107
   *P. perruno* **106-7**
Perruno Catfish **106**
*Phractocephalus* 113
   *P. hemioliopterus 17*, 18, **107**
Pigmy Catfish 70, **77**
Pigmy Suckermouth **94**
*Pimelodella 14*, 15
   *P. cristata* **108**
   *P. geryi* 108
   *P. gracilis* 108
Pimelodidae *14*, 15, *17*, 17, **103-113**
Pimelodids 17, 19, 21, 22, 36, 49, 107
*Pimelodus* 18, 32, 108, 109, 110
   *P. blochi 17*, 18, **108-9**
   *P. clarias* 109
   *P. maculatus 17*, *18*, 18, **109**
   *P. ornatus 17*, 18, **110**
   *P. pictus Copyright page*, *17*, 18, **110**
Piranhas 10
*Platydoras 14*, 15, 86
   *P. costatus* **88**
*Platystacus* 16, 53
Plecs 13, 35
Polka-dot Catfish 18, 109, 110
Porthole Catfish **84**
*Pseudodoras niger 16*, 17, **88**
*Pseudohemiodon laticeps* **98-9**
*Pseudopimelodus* 18
   *P. raninus 17*, **111**, 112
   *P. zungaro* **112**
*Pseudoplatystoma fasciatum 13*, *17*, 19, **112-3**
*Pterophyllum scalare 18*
*Pterygoplichthys* 15, *16*, *48*, 48, 89
   *P. anisitsi* **99**
   *P. gibbiceps* **100**

**R**

Rasboras 58
Rabaut's Catfish **78**
Red Tail Catfish 18, 22, *36*, 36, 37, **107**
*Rineloricaria 14*, 15, 22, 44, 47, 90
   *R. fallax* 101
   *R. lanceolata 18*, **100**, 101
   *R. lima* **101**

*R. stewarti* 101
Royal Plec 15, **95**

**S**

Sailfin Catfishes 18
Sailfin Pim 18, **104**, *105*
Sailfin Plec 15, **100**
Salt and Pepper Catfish **69**
Scaleless Catfishes 15
Shark Catfish *17*, 17, 52, **53**
Shovel-nosed Catfish 18, 19, 37, **113**
Silver Dollars 100
Skunk Catfish **66**
Snow King Plec 15, **99**, 100
*Sorubim lima 17*, *18*, 18, 19, *50-1*, **113**
Spade Catfish **98**
Spoon-head Whiptail **93**
Spotted Catfish **65**, **72**
Spotted Pim **109**
Spotted Talking Catfishes 48, **86**
Striped Plec **97**, 98
*Sturisoma 16*, 16, 47, 90
   *S. aureum* 18, **102**, 103
   *S. panamese* 102
   *S. barbatum 102*, 102, **103**
Suckermouth Catfishes 13, *14*, *16*, 22, 47, 89, 91, 93
Sychr's Catfish **81**

**T**

Talking Catfishes *14*, 15, *16*, 32, 33, 56, 86
Tail Spot Pigmy Catfish **70**
*Tatia* 14, 15
   *T. aulopygia* **57**
Tetras 10, 15, 18, 58
Thorny Catfishes 56, 86
Three Line Catfish **83**
Tiger Catfish 19, 22, 36, 37, **112**
*Trachelyichthys 14*, 15, 33
   *T. decaradiatus* **58**
   *T. exilis* 58
*Trachelyopterichthys taeniatus* **58**, *59*
*Trachysurus* 17
Twig Catfish 13, 16, 22, **90**

**W**

Whiptail Catfish **100**
Whiptail Catfishes 13, *14*, 15, *16*, 22, 35, 44, 47, 89
Winged Driftwood **54**

**Z**

Zamora Catfish 17

# Picture credits

**Artists**
Copyright of the artwork illustrations on the pages following the artist's name is the property of Salamander Books Ltd.

Rod Ferring: 14, 16, 17, 19

Craig Greenwood: 46

Guy Troughton: 12-13, 21, 24-5, 26, 32-3, 37, 44-5

**Photographs**
The publishers wish to thank the following photographers and agencies who have supplied photographs for this book. The photographs have been credited by page number and position on the page: (B)Bottom, (T)Top, (C)Centre, (BL)Bottom left etc.

David Allison: 85, 96-7(T), 102(B), 108-9(T), 112-3(B)

Jan-Eric Larsson: 50-1, 75(T), 84(T)

Chris Mattison: 31(T)

Arend van den Nieuwenhuizen: 23(B), 30-1(B), 46, 47, 53, 64-5(B), 65(T), 67(B), 72-3(T), 73(B), 78, 79(B), 81(T), 82(B), 86, 88(T), 89, 94-5(T), 101(T), 102(T), 104-5(B), 106(T), 111(B)

Mike Sandford: 87, 88(B), 91(B), 95(B)

David Sands: 23(T), 28, 34, 35, 36, 41, 48, 52, 54, 55, 56, 57, 58, 59, 60, 61, 63, 64(T), 66, 67(T), 68, 69, 70, 71, 72(B), 74, 75(B), 76, 77, 79(T), 80, 81(B), 82(T), 83, 84(B), 90, 91(T), 92(B), 93(B), 94(B), 96(B), 97(B), 98, 100, 101(B), 103, 104(T), 105(T), 106-7(B), 107(T), 108(B), 109(B), 110, 111(T), 112(T), 113(T)

Uwe Werner: 10-11, 92-3(T), 99

**Acknowledgements**
The author wishes to thank the following people for their help in preparing this book: Bruce Clarke, Stuart Rogers, Dr Gerlof Mees, Heiko Bleher and Dr Walter Foersch.

*Brochis britskii,* Brazil